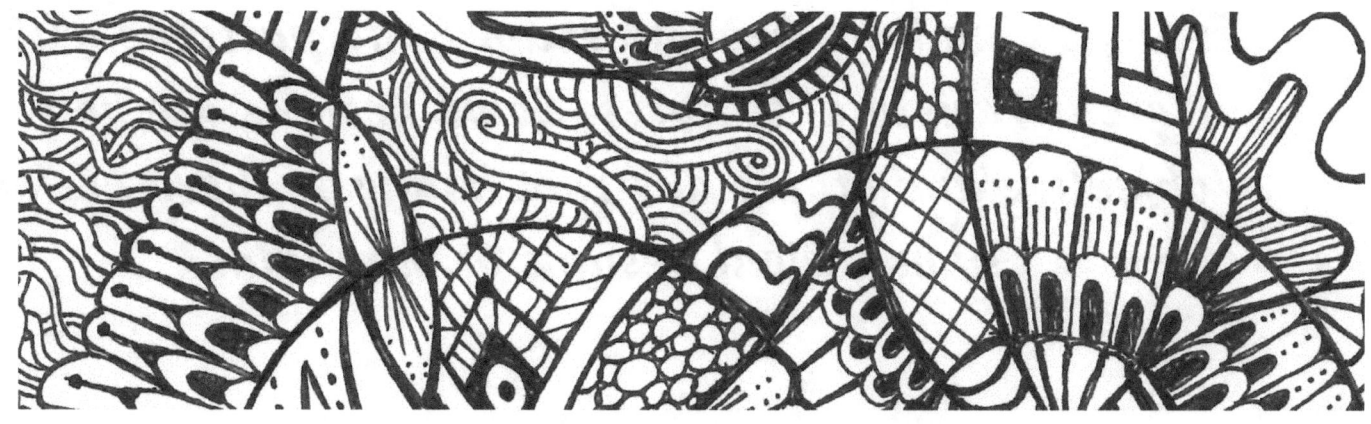

COLORING BOOK

For Adults

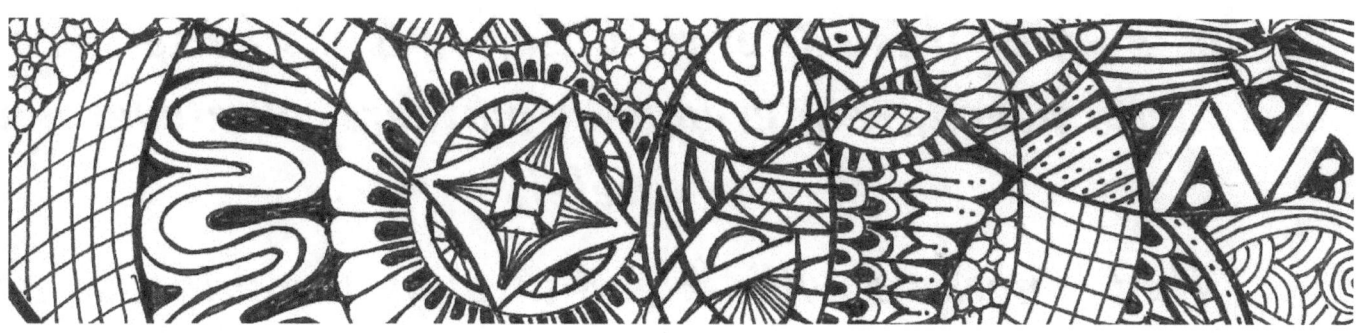

Fifty hand-drawn designs for you to color and enjoy.

By Ten Zone Designs

This coloring book features 50 unique, original designs. Free-flowing lines become shapes and patterns with a great variety of textures. Some designs are non-objective and others abstract images. There are no symmetrical designs or mandalas.

Many of the drawings are simple, easy coloring while others are complex and involved. If the image has many tiny pieces to color, you may want to group together shapes with similar textures or patterns and color them as a unit. It is easier and it often looks better. Color with pencil, pen, crayon or markers, whatever you prefer.

Hint: markers could bleed through the page, so you may wish to place a sheet of paper or poster board under your work to protect the next drawing.

Color it as YOU see it. Relax ... enjoy the experience.

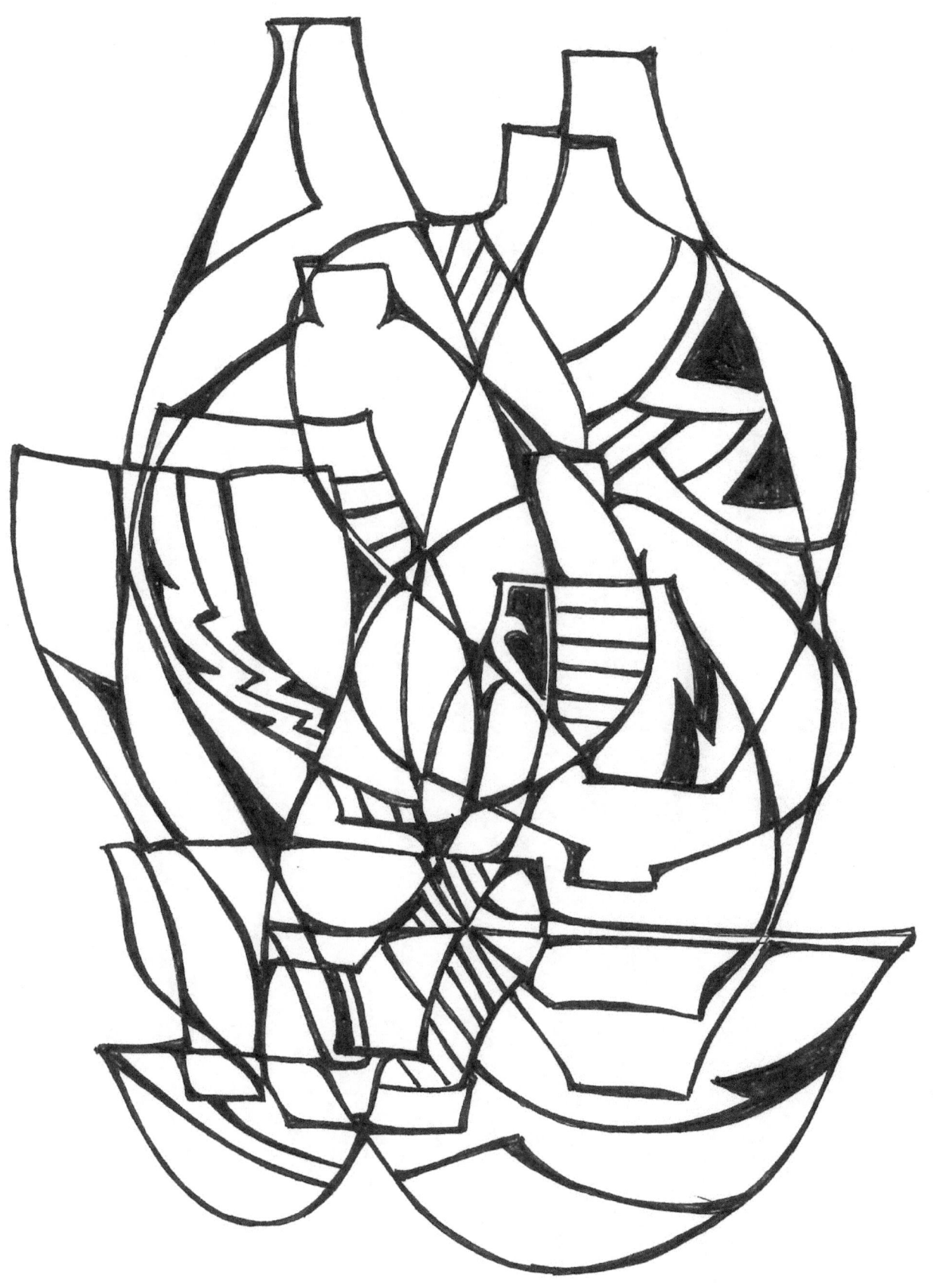

You may wish to place a sheet of paper or poster board under the page you are coloring to prevent damaging the next image.

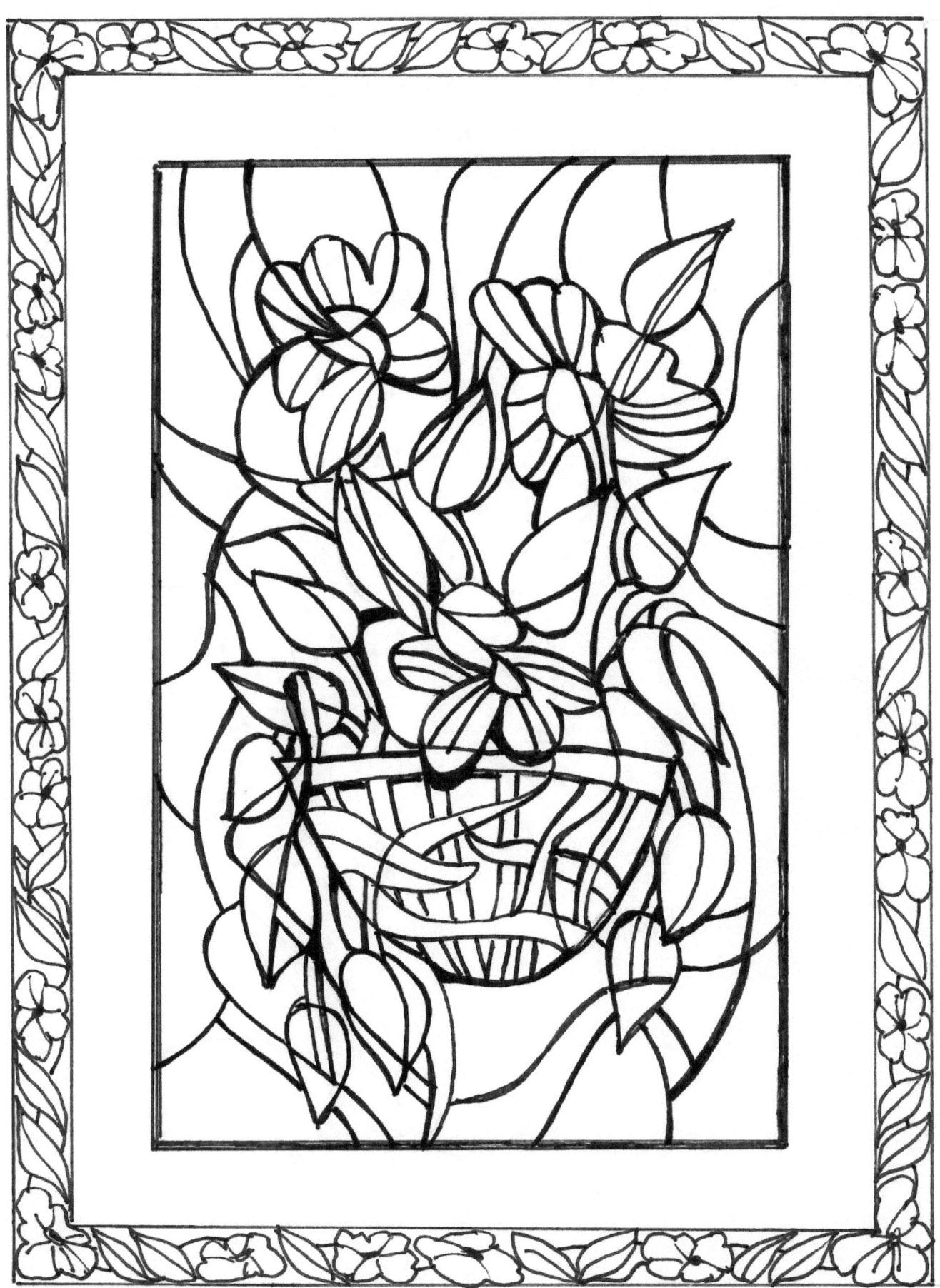

You may wish to place a sheet of paper or poster board under the page you are coloring to prevent damaging the next image.

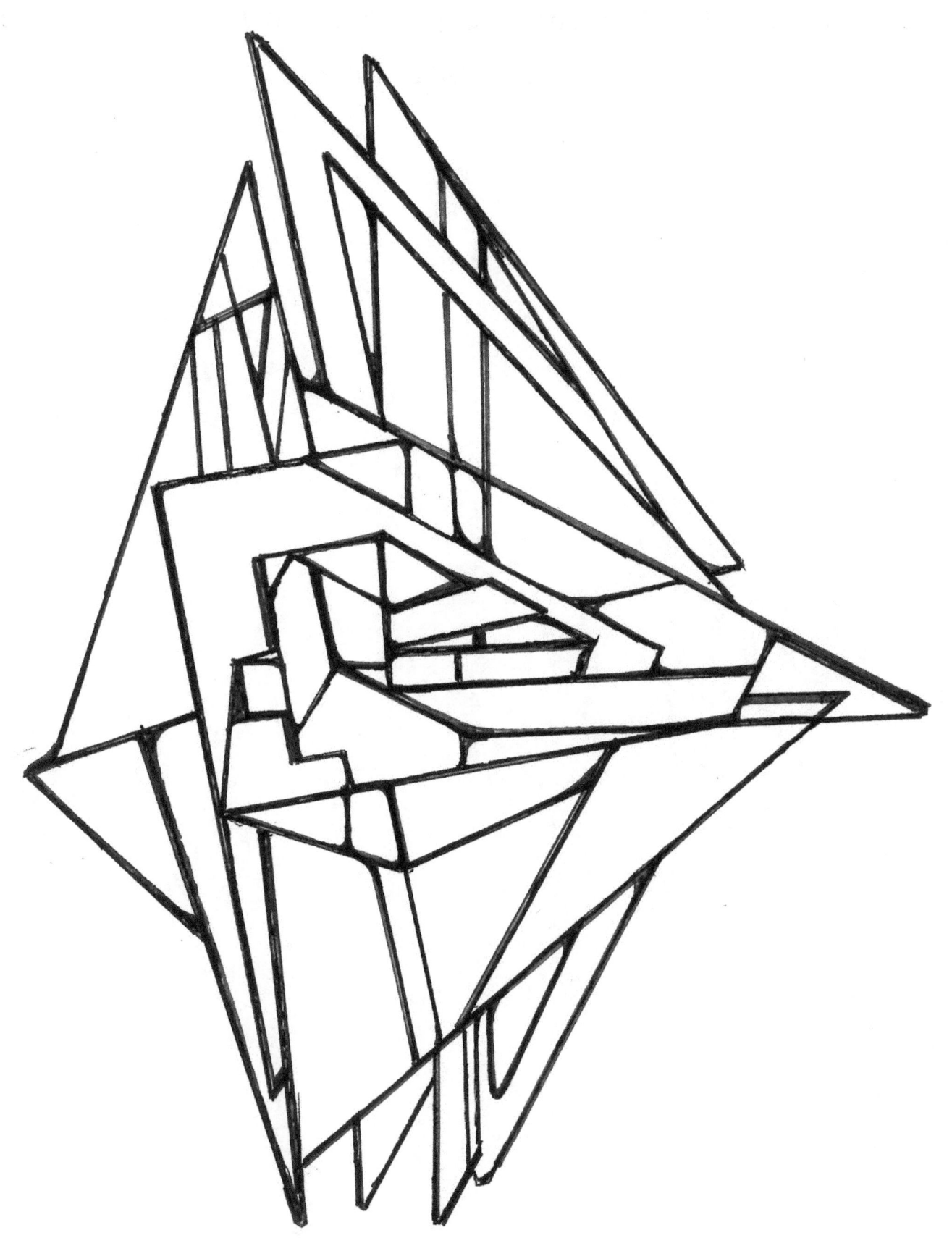

You may wish to place a sheet of paper or poster board under the page you are coloring to prevent damaging the next image.

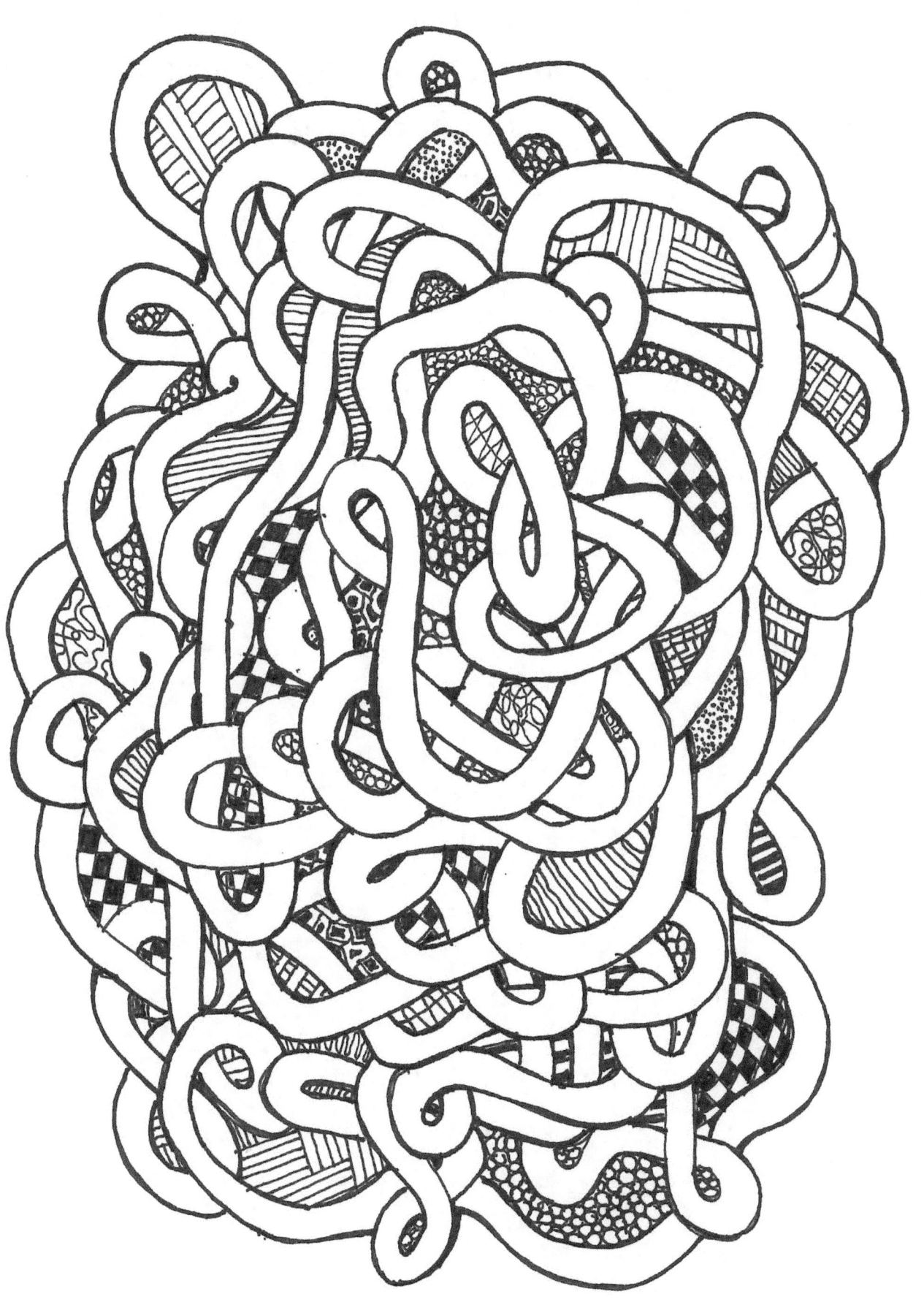

You may wish to place a sheet of paper or poster board under the page you are coloring to prevent damaging the next image.

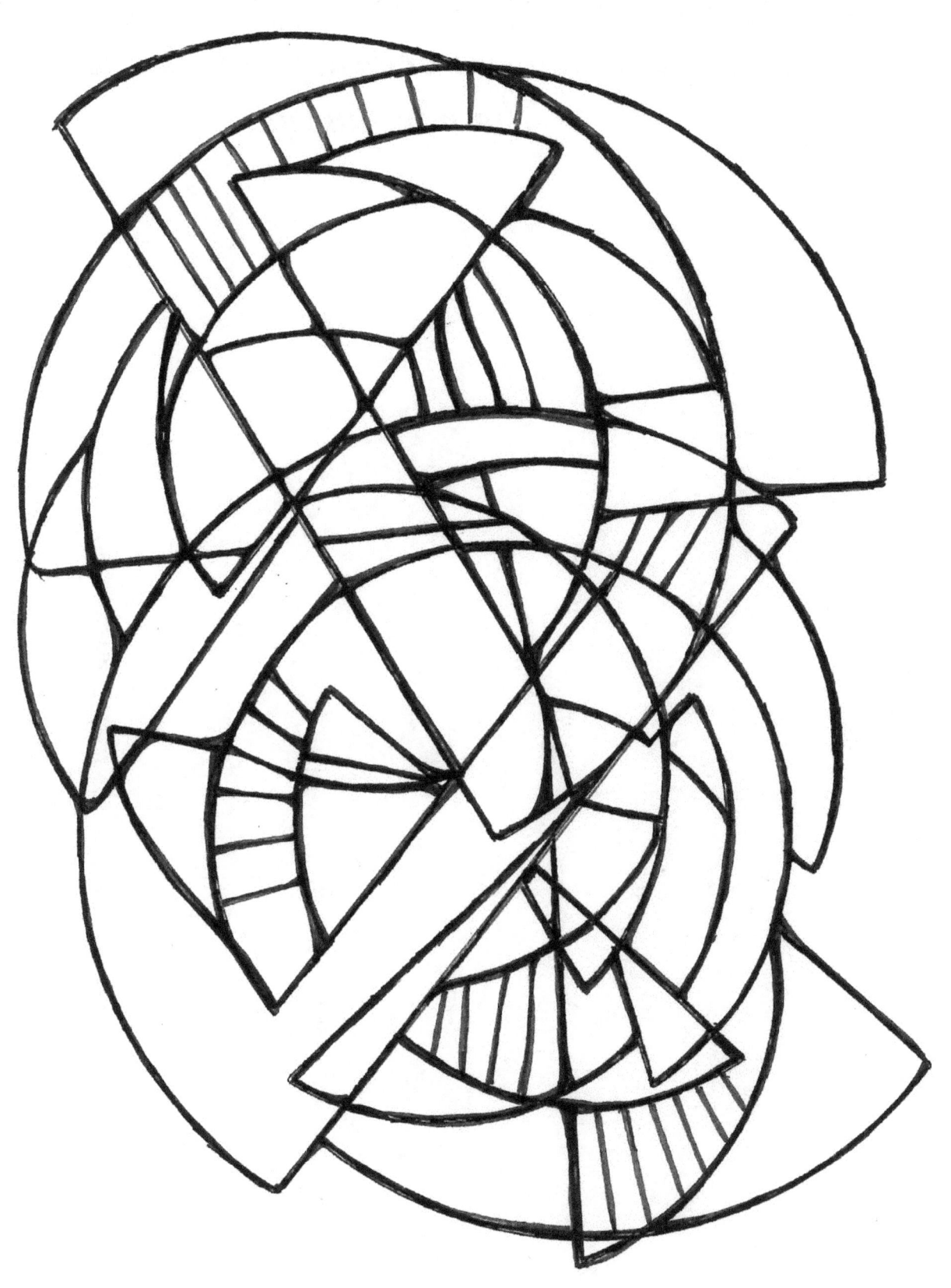

You may wish to place a sheet of paper or poster board under the page you are coloring to prevent damaging the next image.

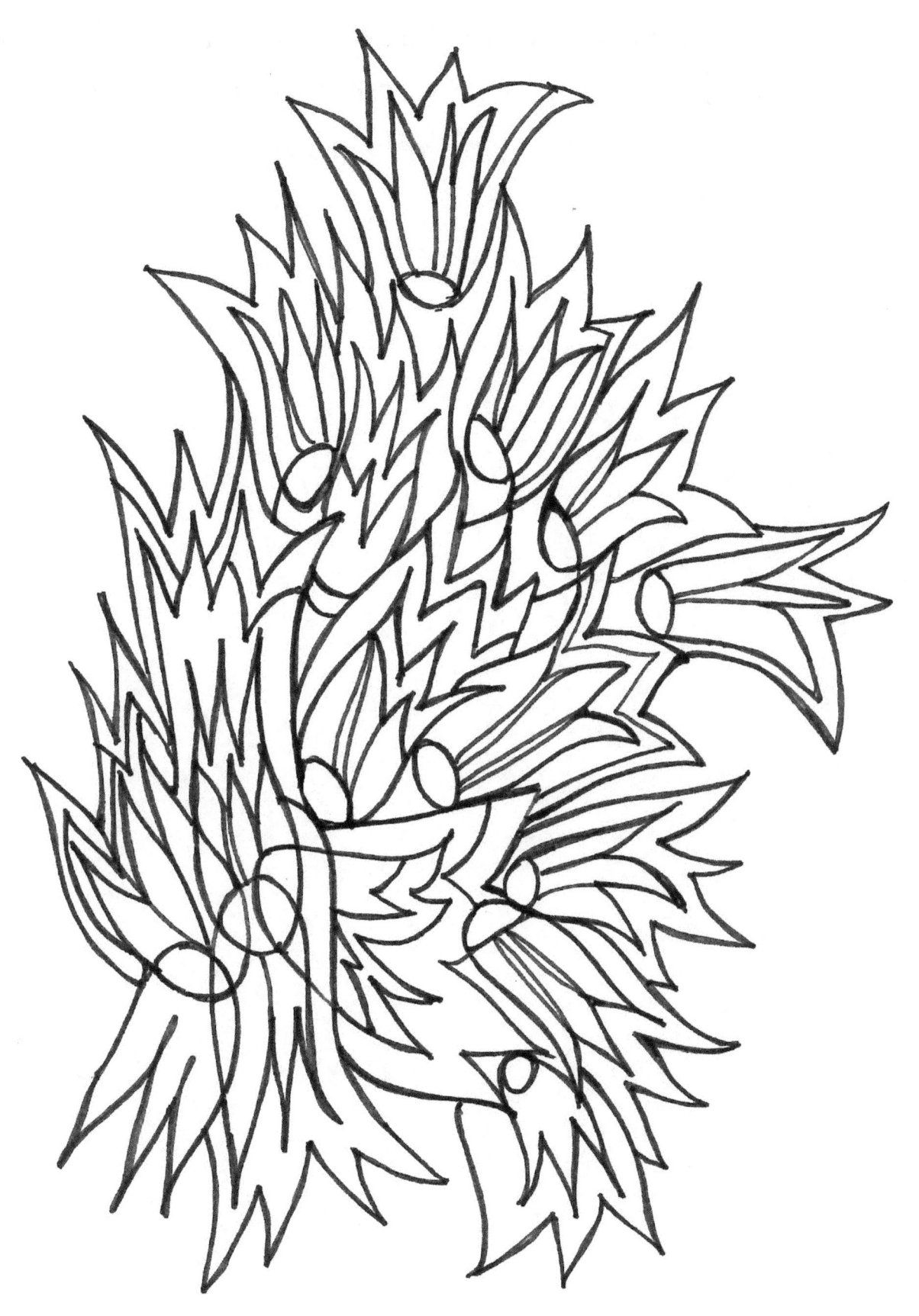

You may wish to place a sheet of paper or poster board under the page you are coloring to prevent damaging the next image.

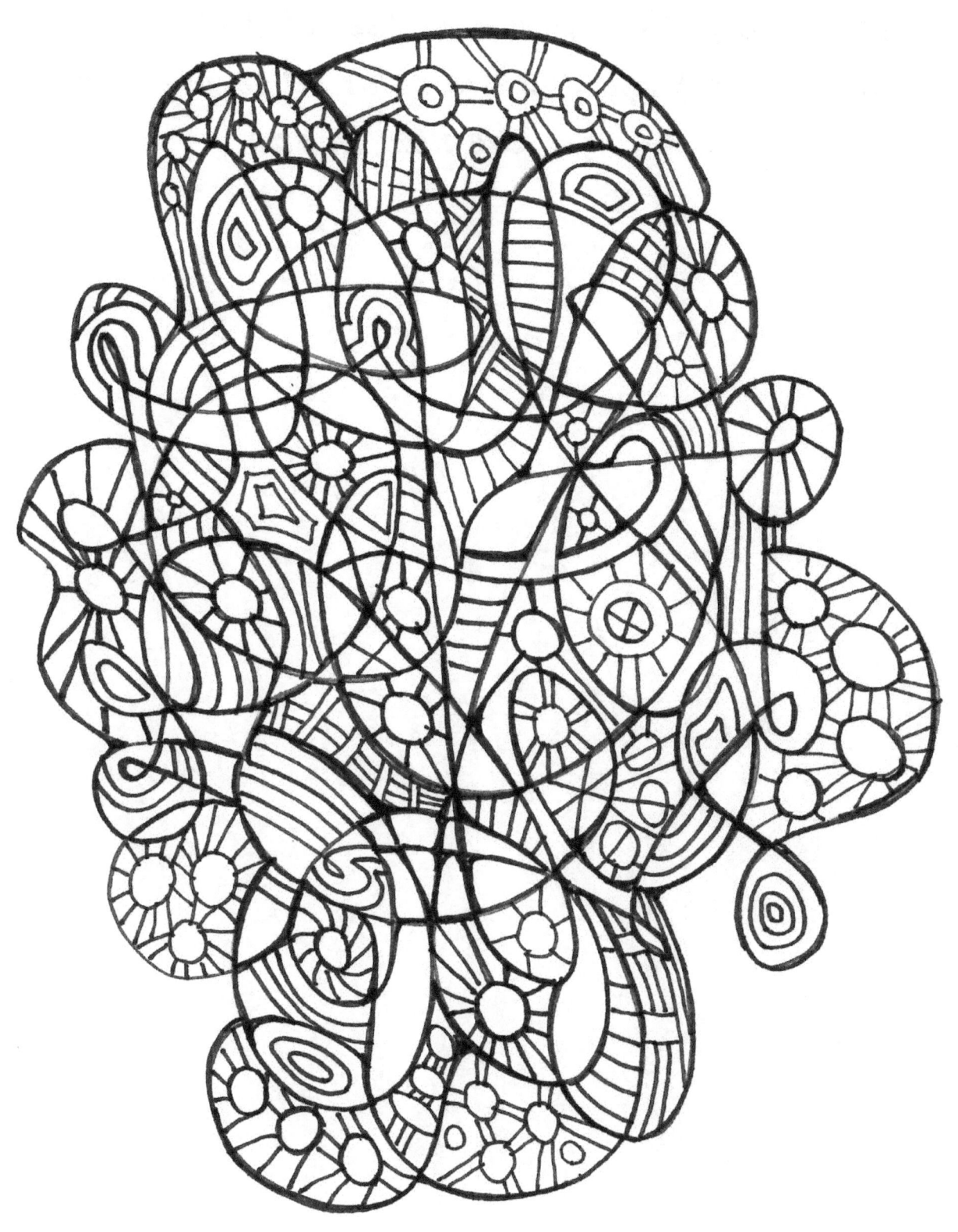

You may wish to place a sheet of paper or poster board under the page you are coloring to prevent damaging the next image.

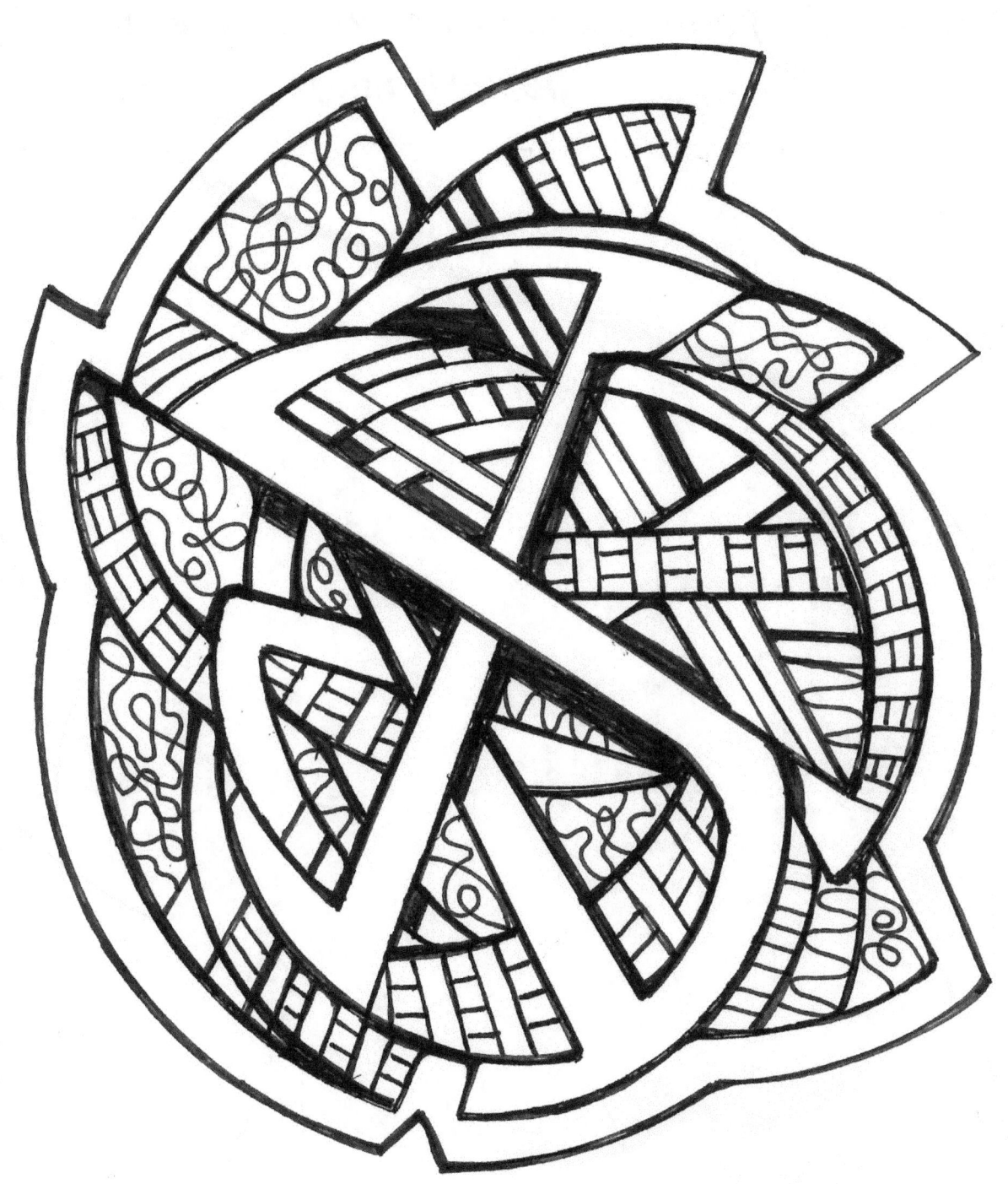

You may wish to place a sheet of paper or poster board under the page you are coloring to prevent damaging the next image.

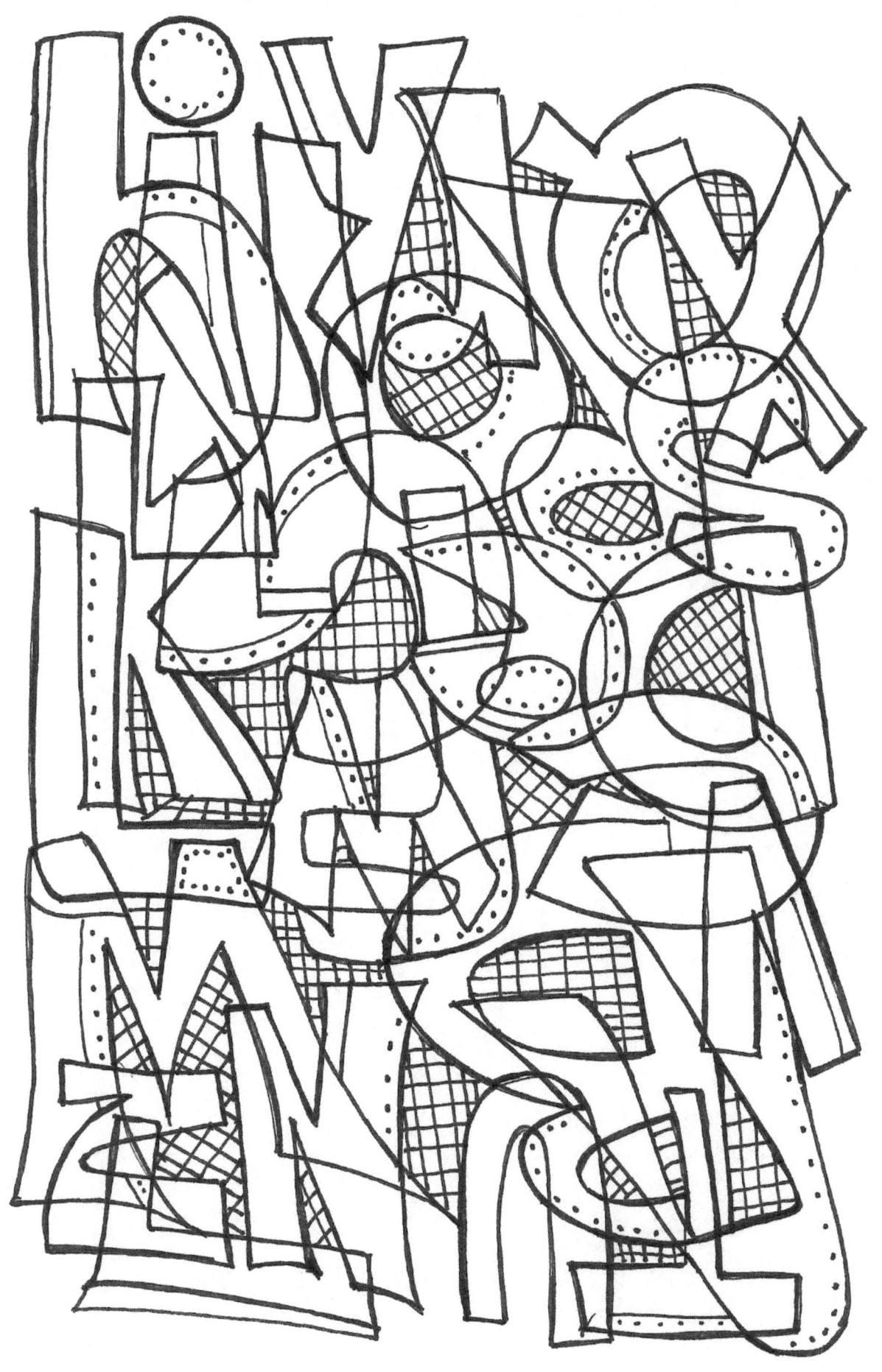

You may wish to place a sheet of paper or poster board under the page you are coloring to prevent damaging the next image.

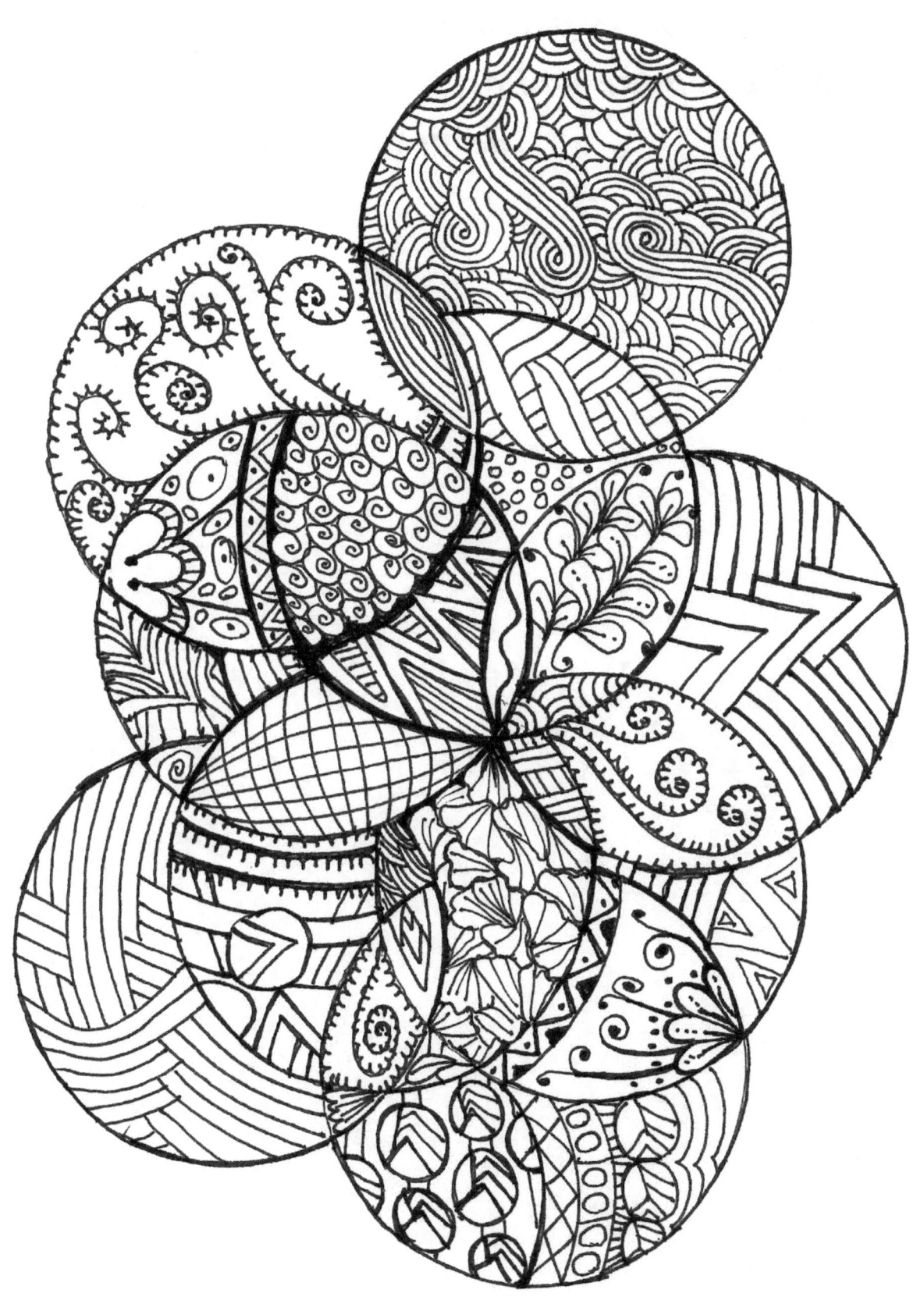

You may wish to place a sheet of paper or poster board under the page you are coloring to prevent damaging the next image.

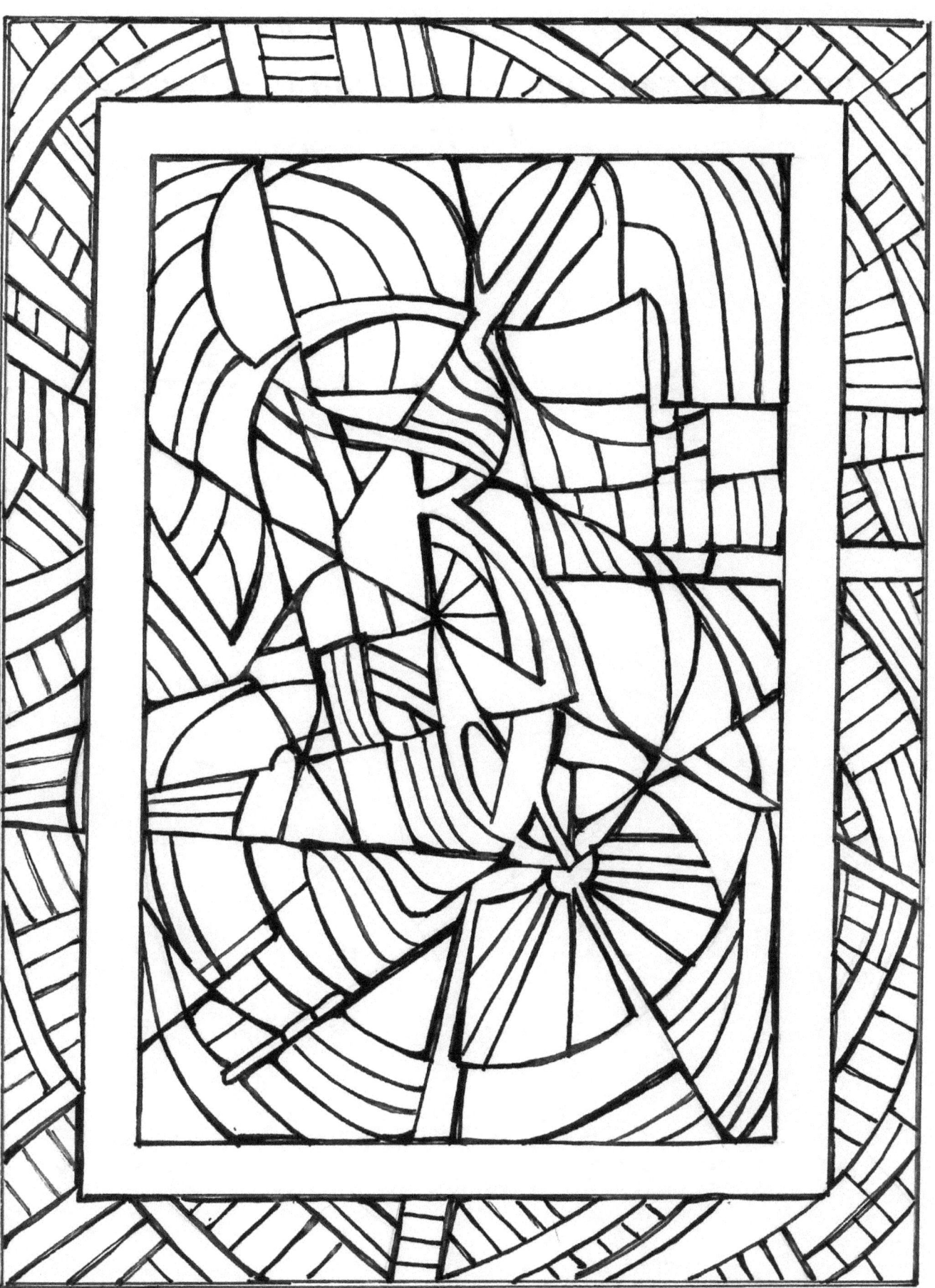

You may wish to place a sheet of paper or poster board under the page you are coloring to prevent damaging the next image.

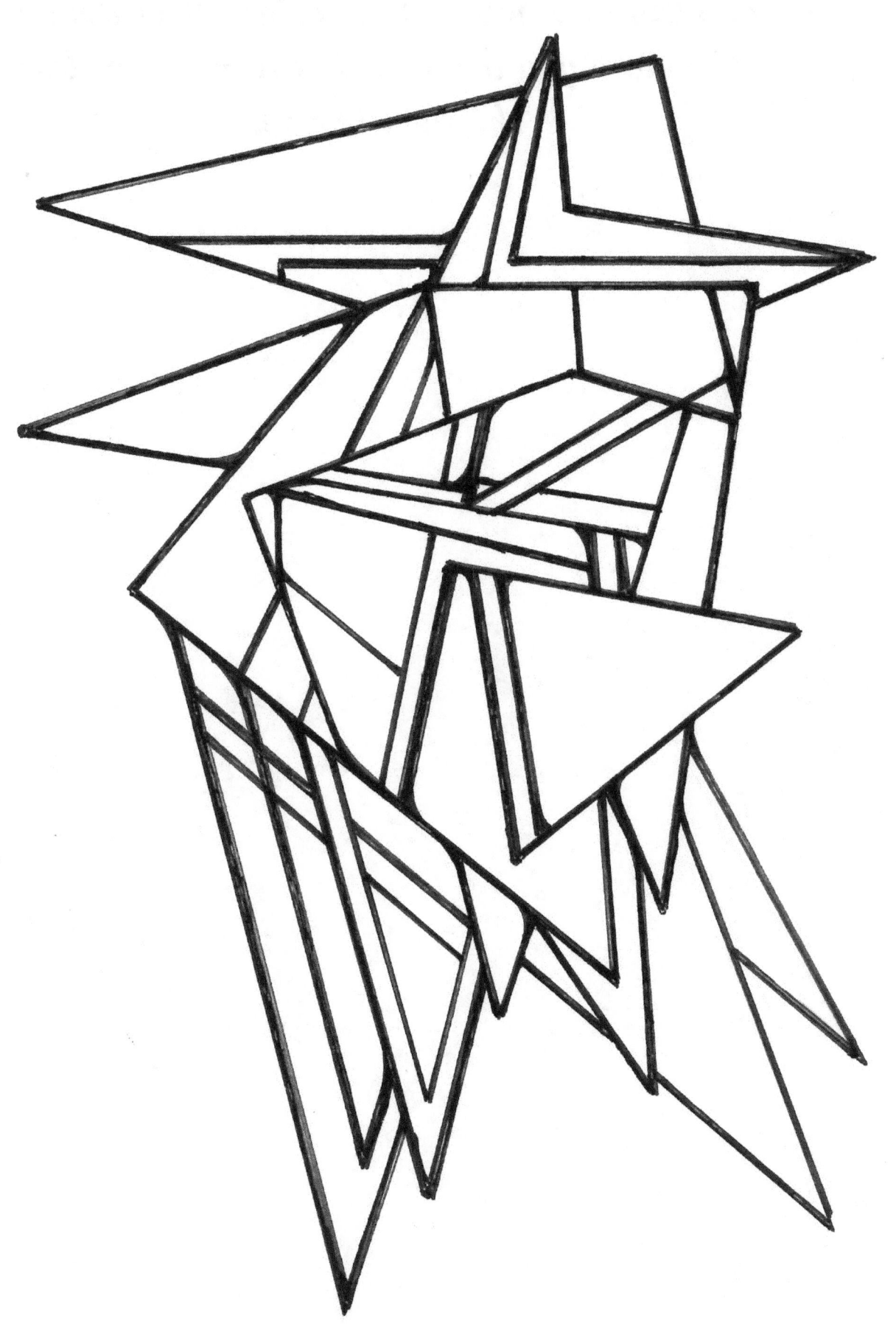

You may wish to place a sheet of paper or poster board under the page you are coloring to prevent damaging the next image.

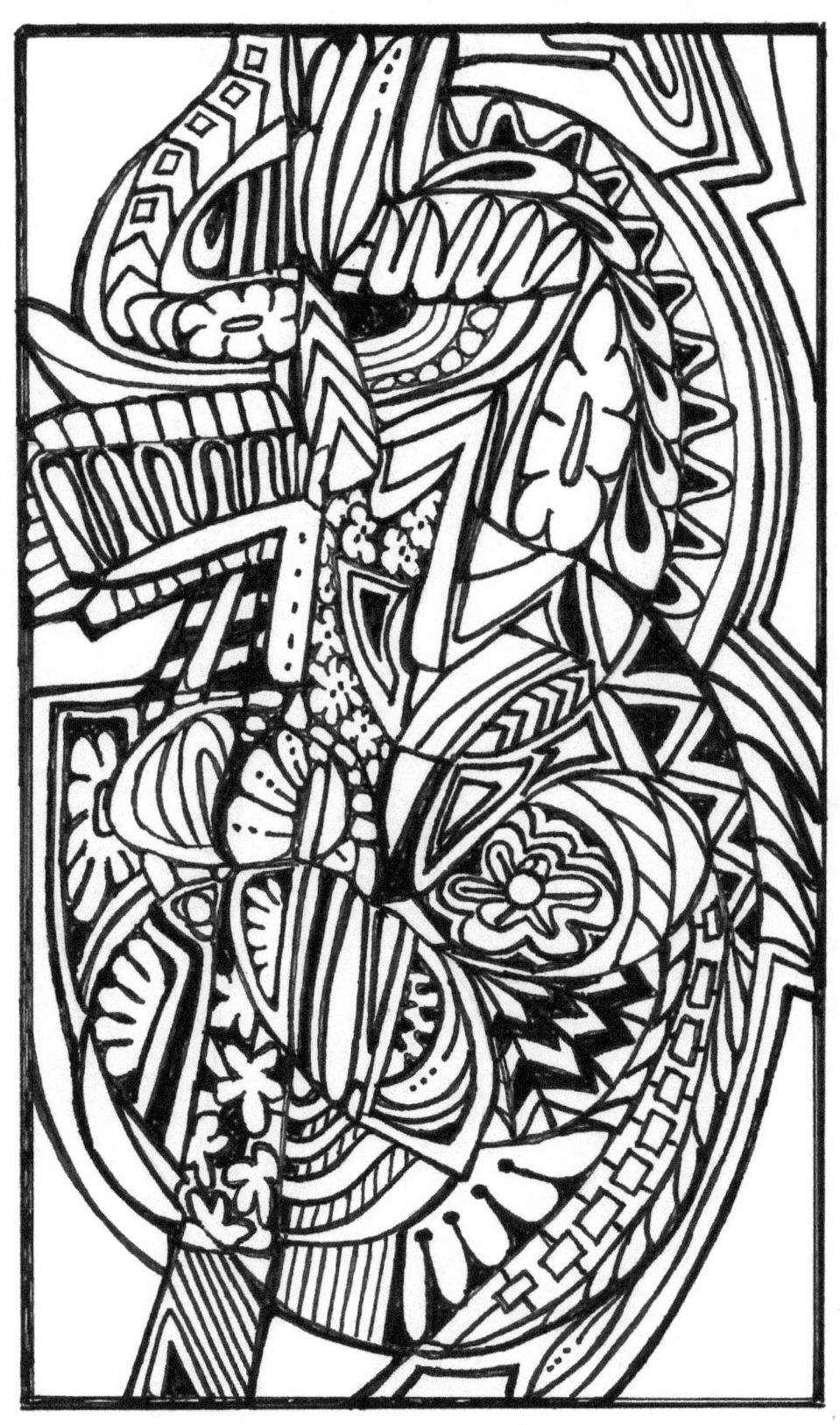

You may wish to place a sheet of paper or poster board under the page you are coloring to prevent damaging the next image.

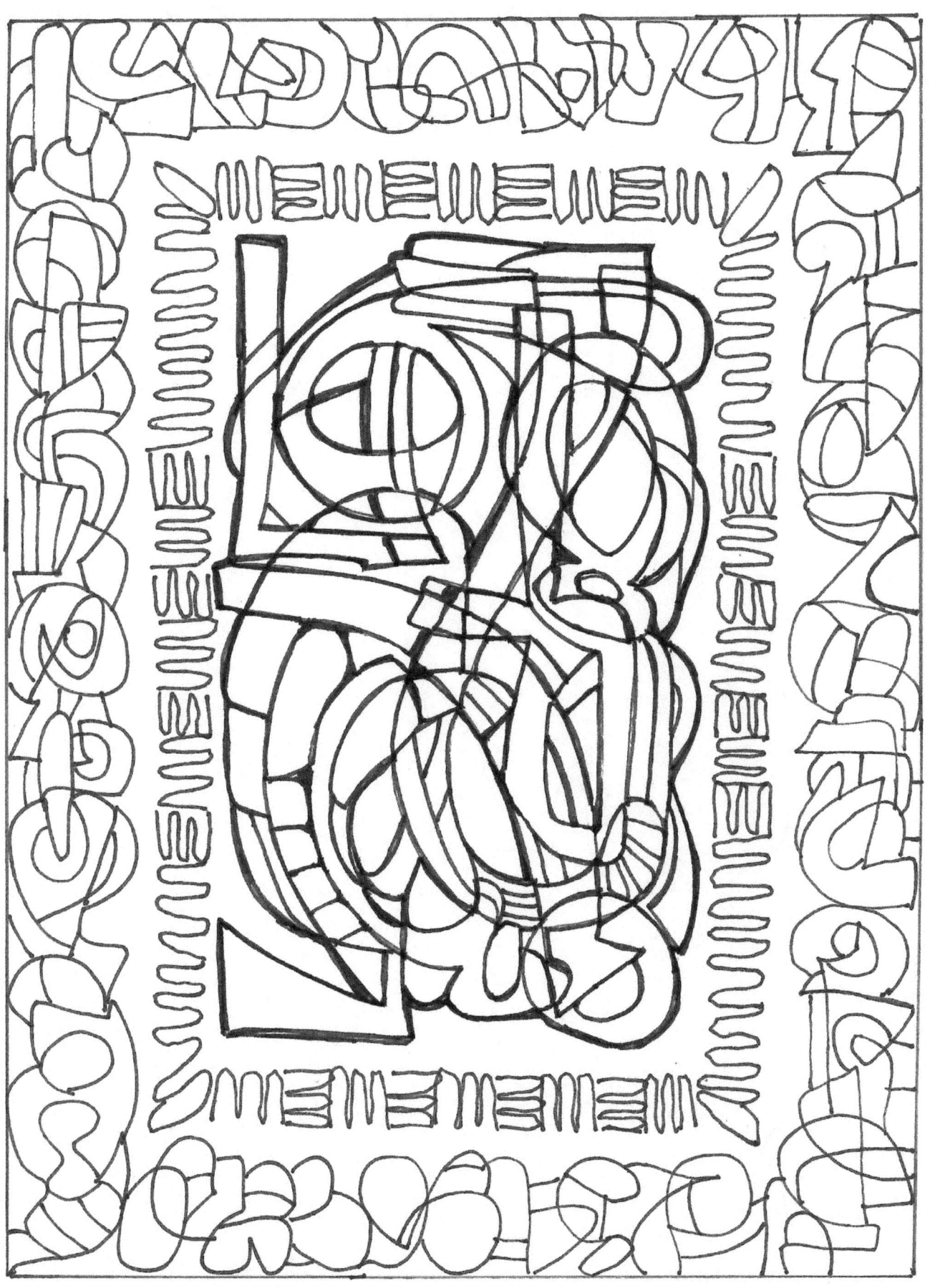

You may wish to place a sheet of paper or poster board under the page you are coloring to prevent damaging the next image.

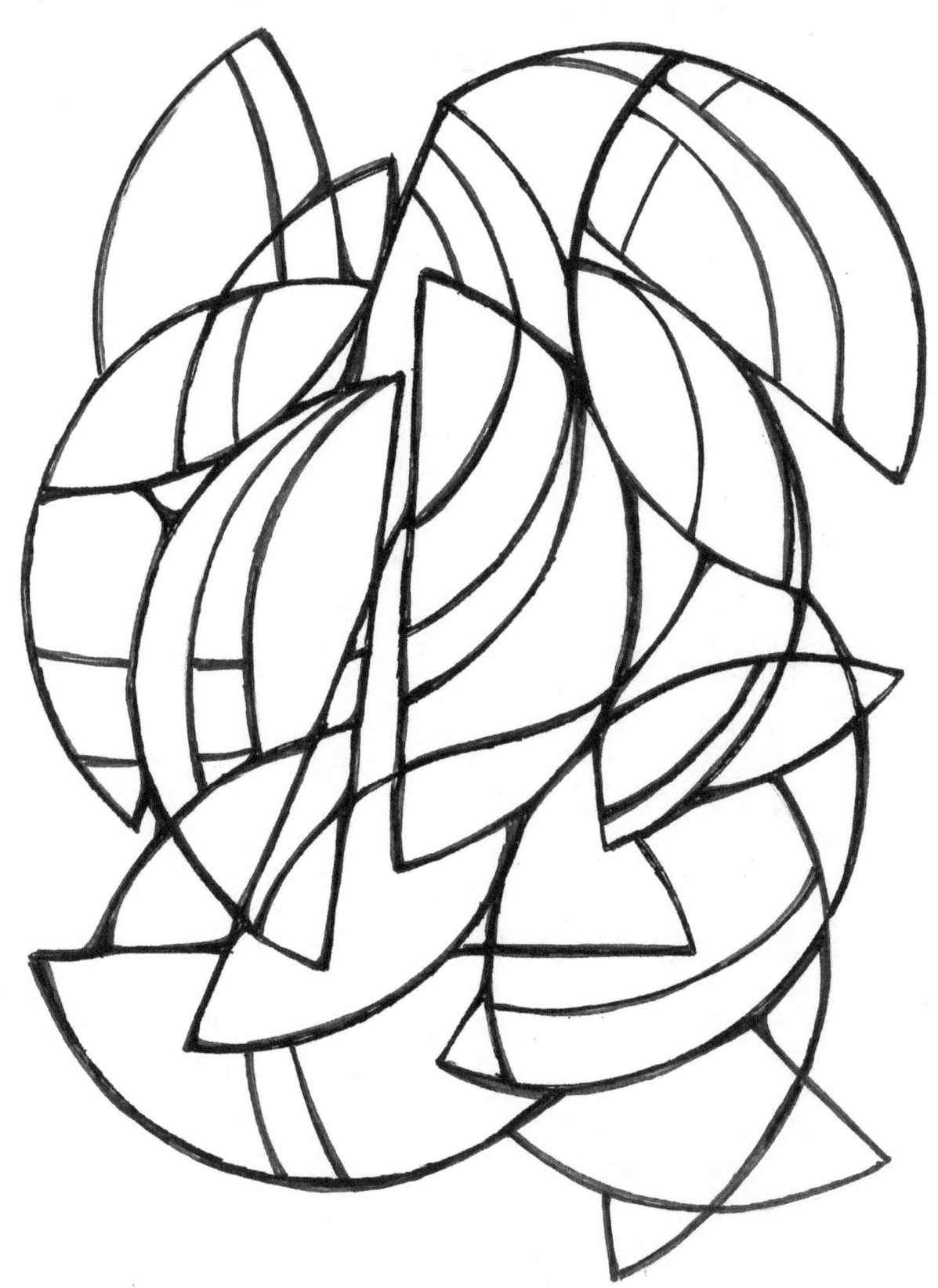

You may wish to place a sheet of paper or poster board under the page you are coloring to prevent damaging the next image.

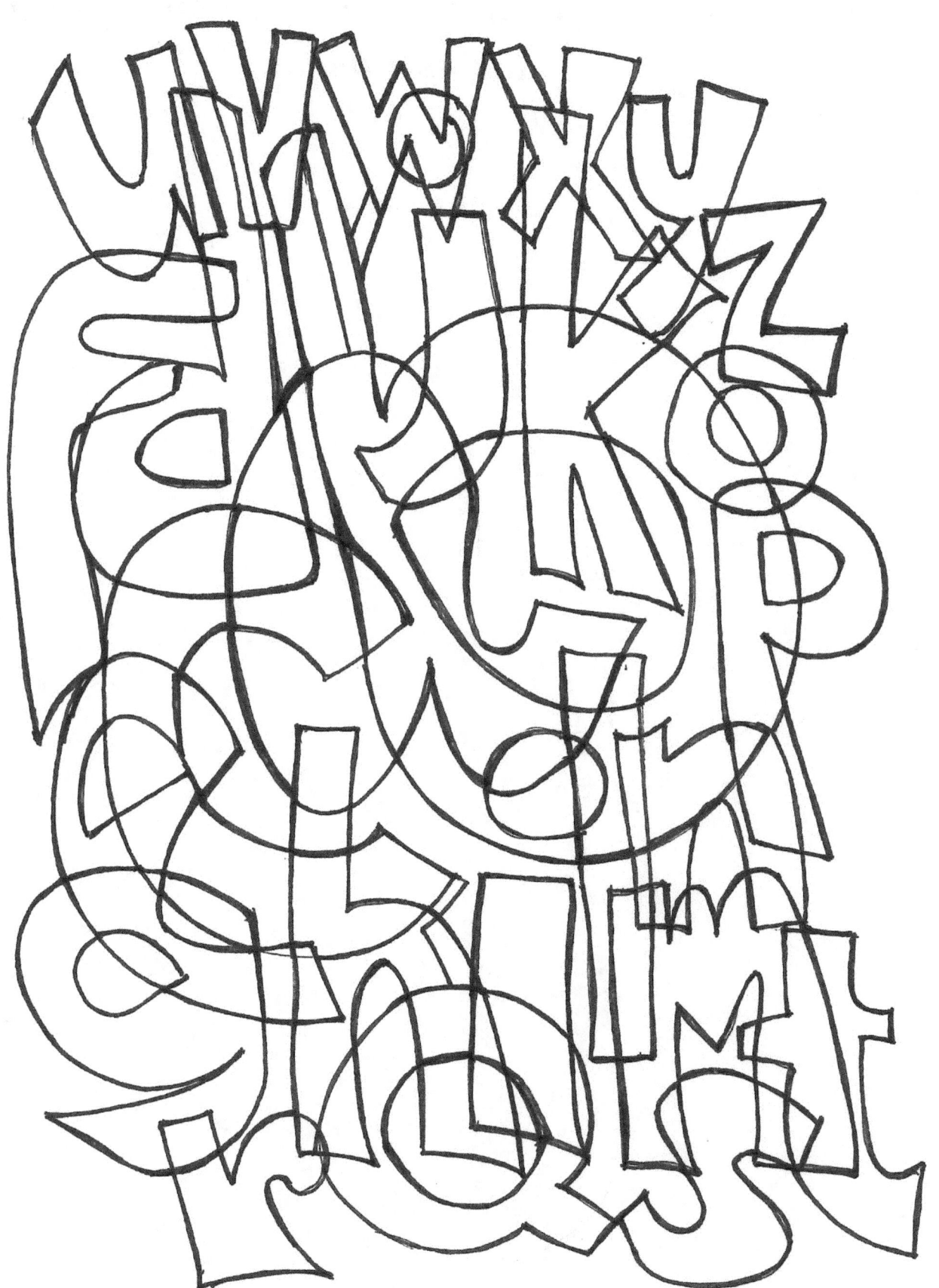

You may wish to place a sheet of paper or poster board under the page you are coloring to prevent damaging the next image.

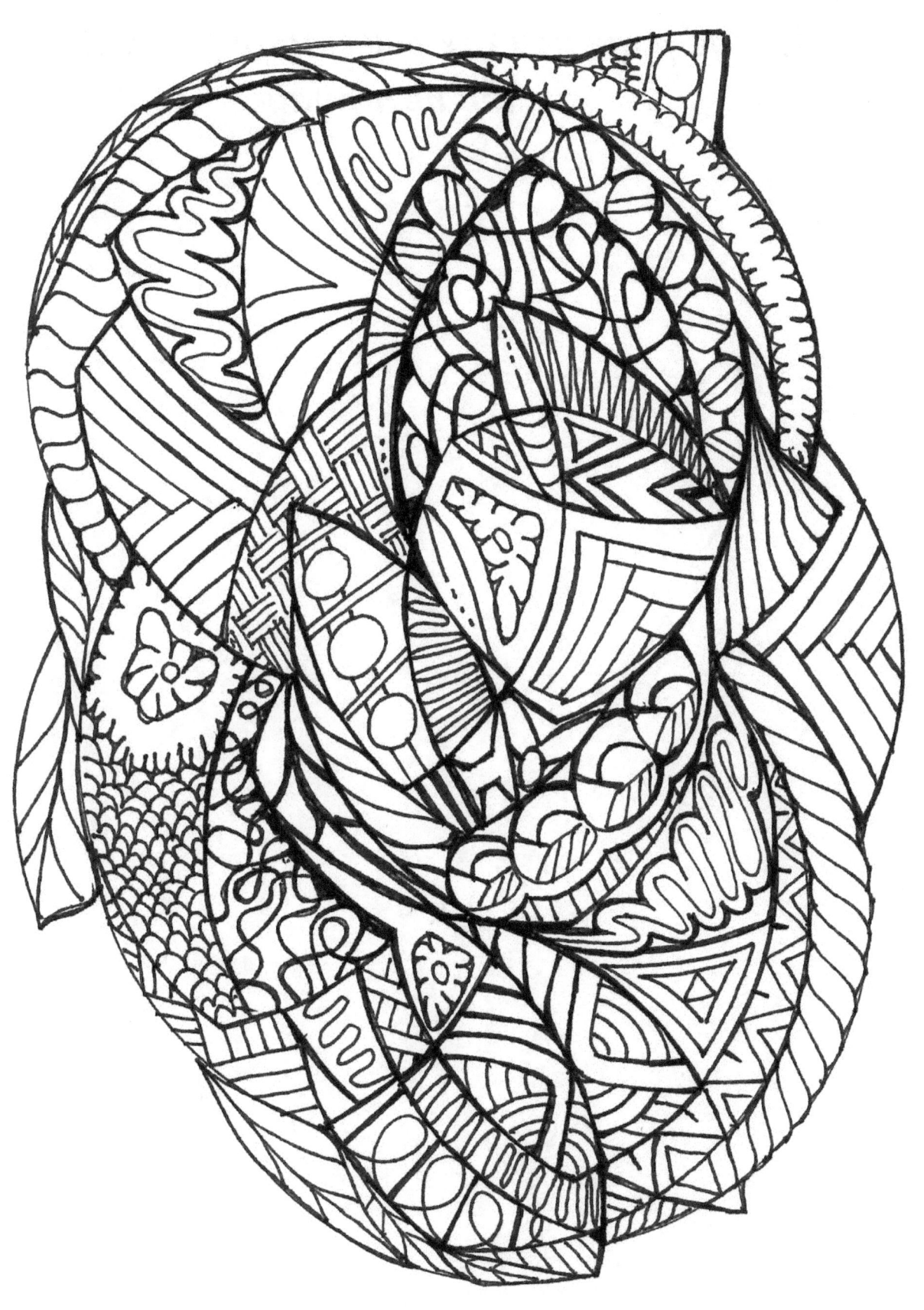

You may wish to place a sheet of paper or poster board under the page you are coloring to prevent damaging the next image.

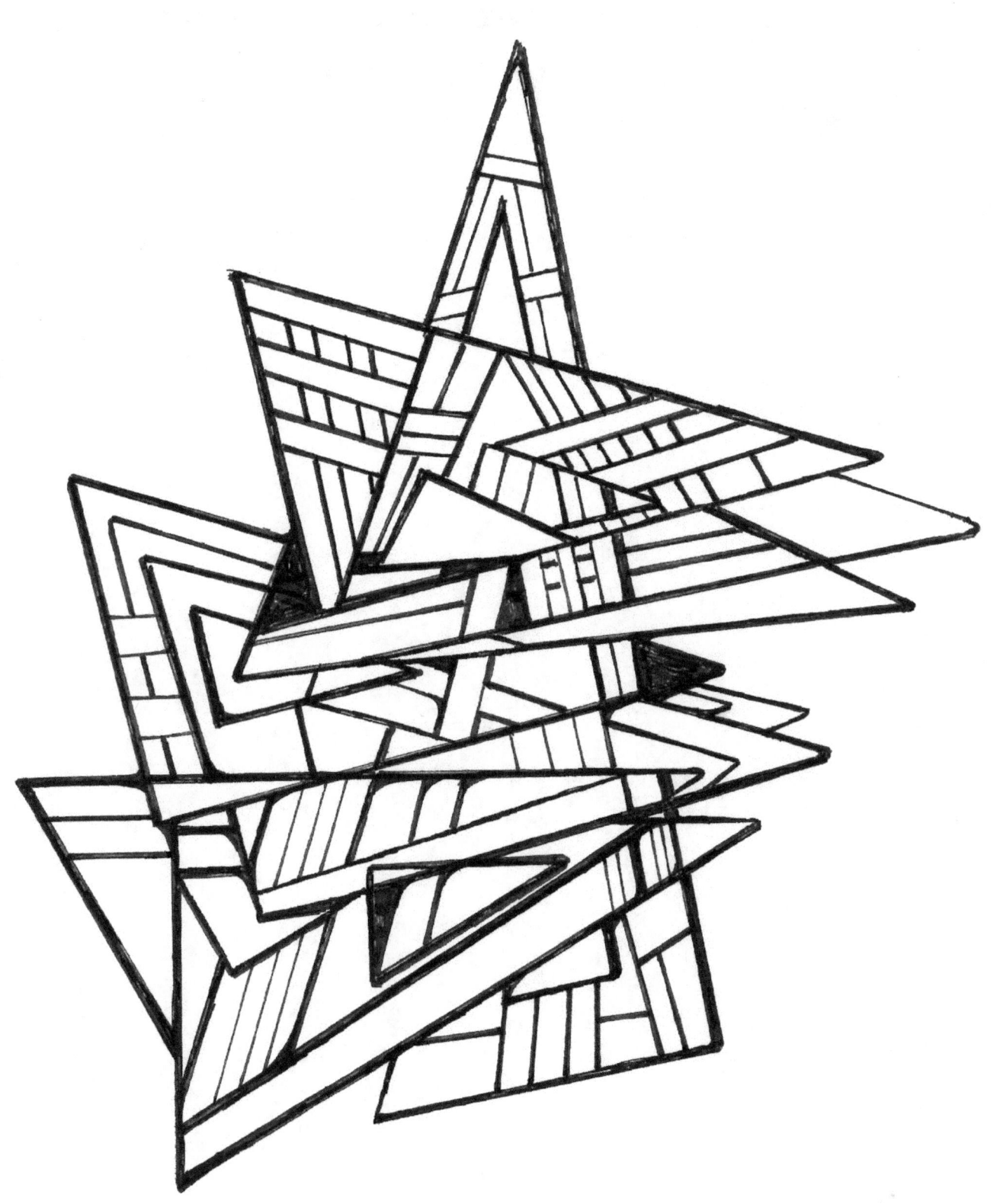

You may wish to place a sheet of paper or poster board under the page you are coloring to prevent damaging the next image.

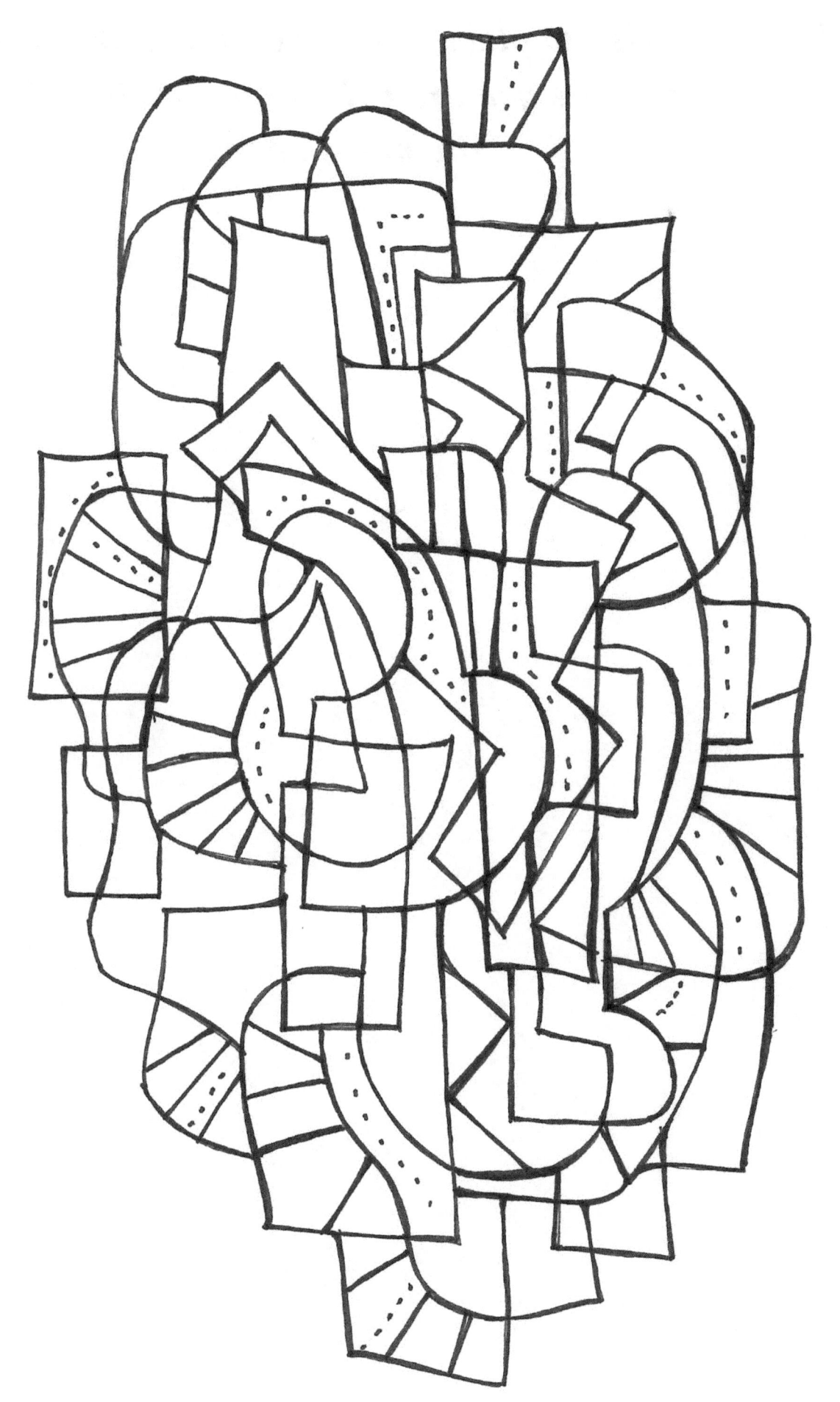

You may wish to place a sheet of paper or poster board under the page you are coloring to prevent damaging the next image.

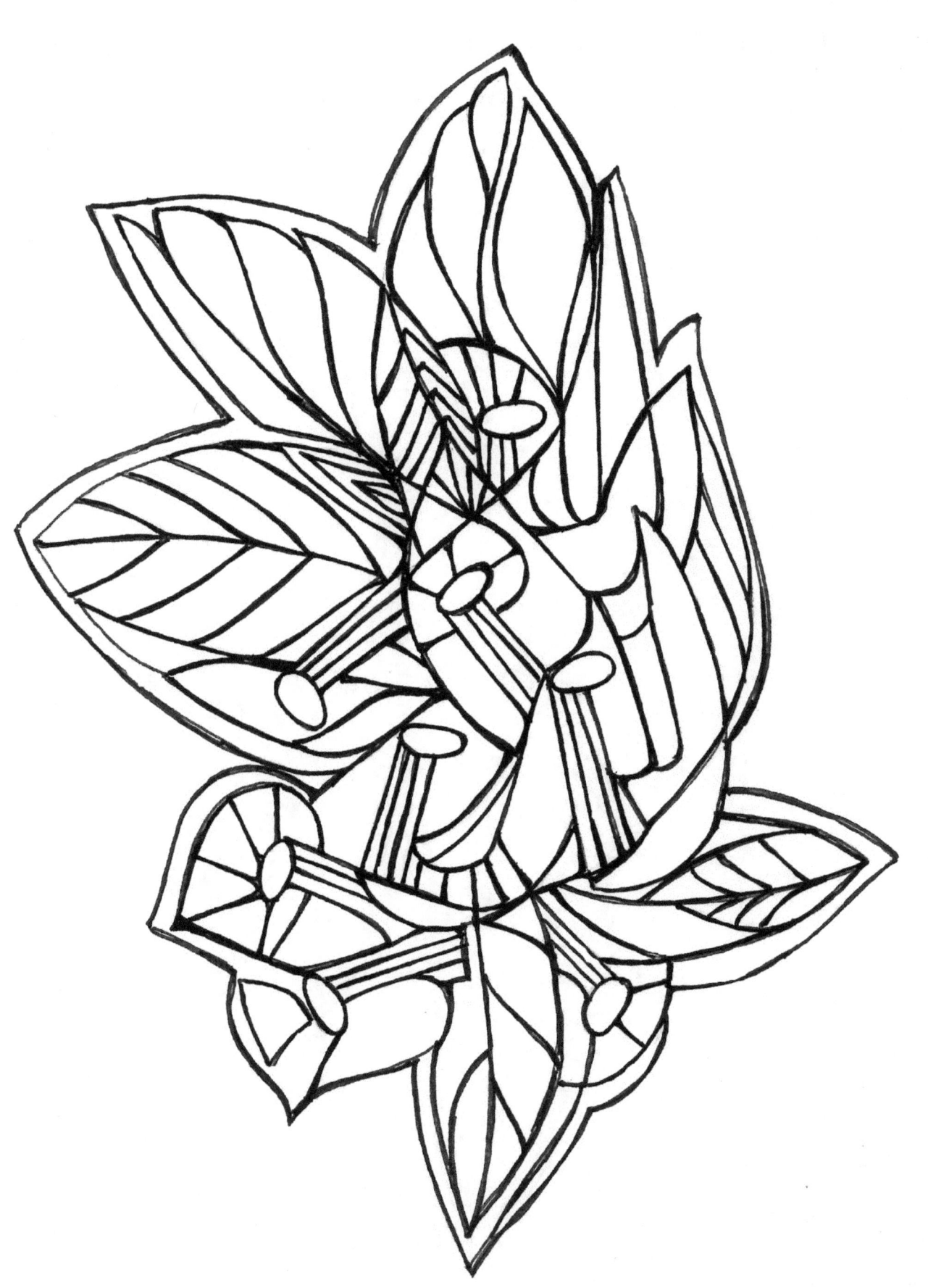

You may wish to place a sheet of paper or poster board under the page you are coloring to prevent damaging the next image.

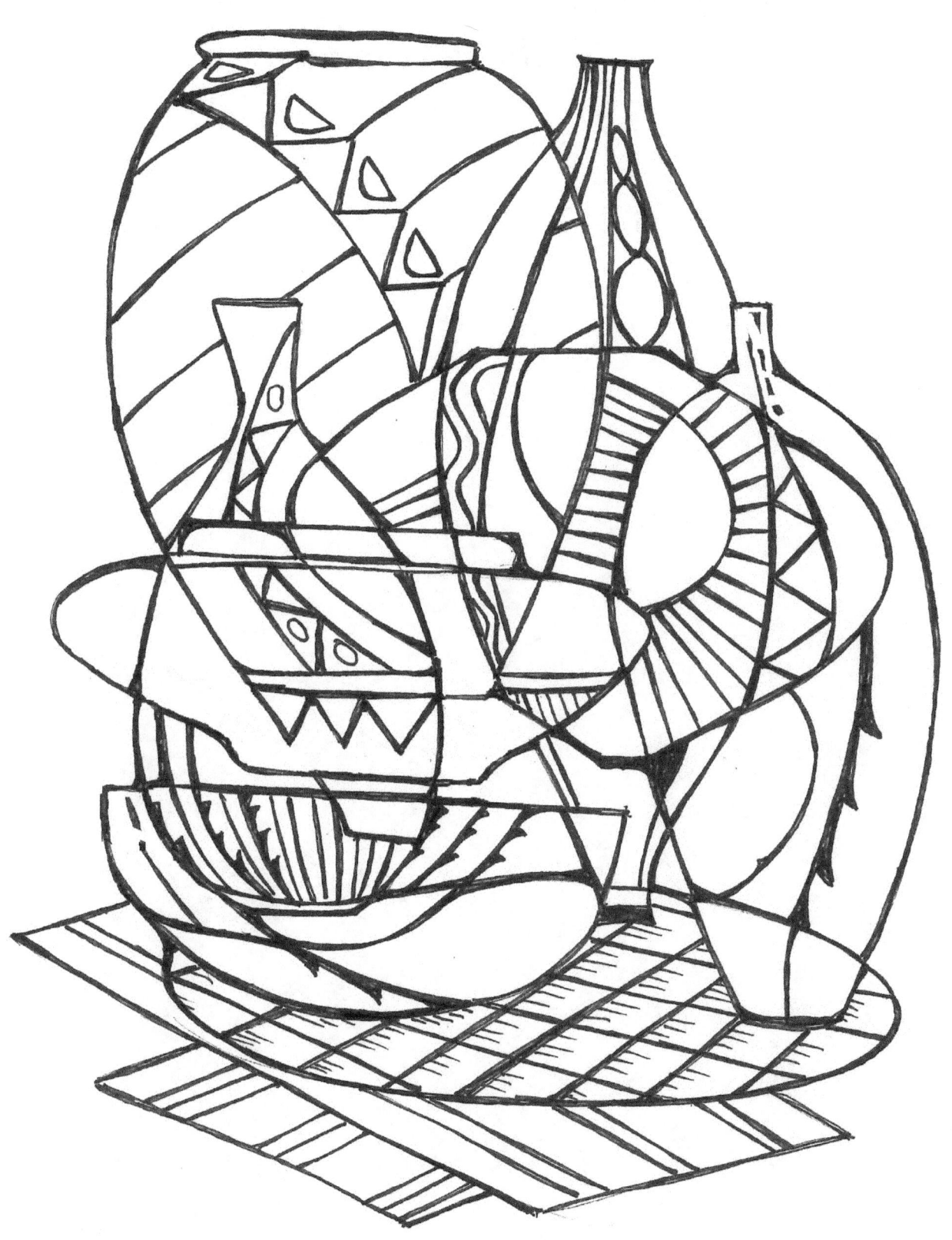

You may wish to place a sheet of paper or poster board under the page you are coloring to prevent damaging the next image.

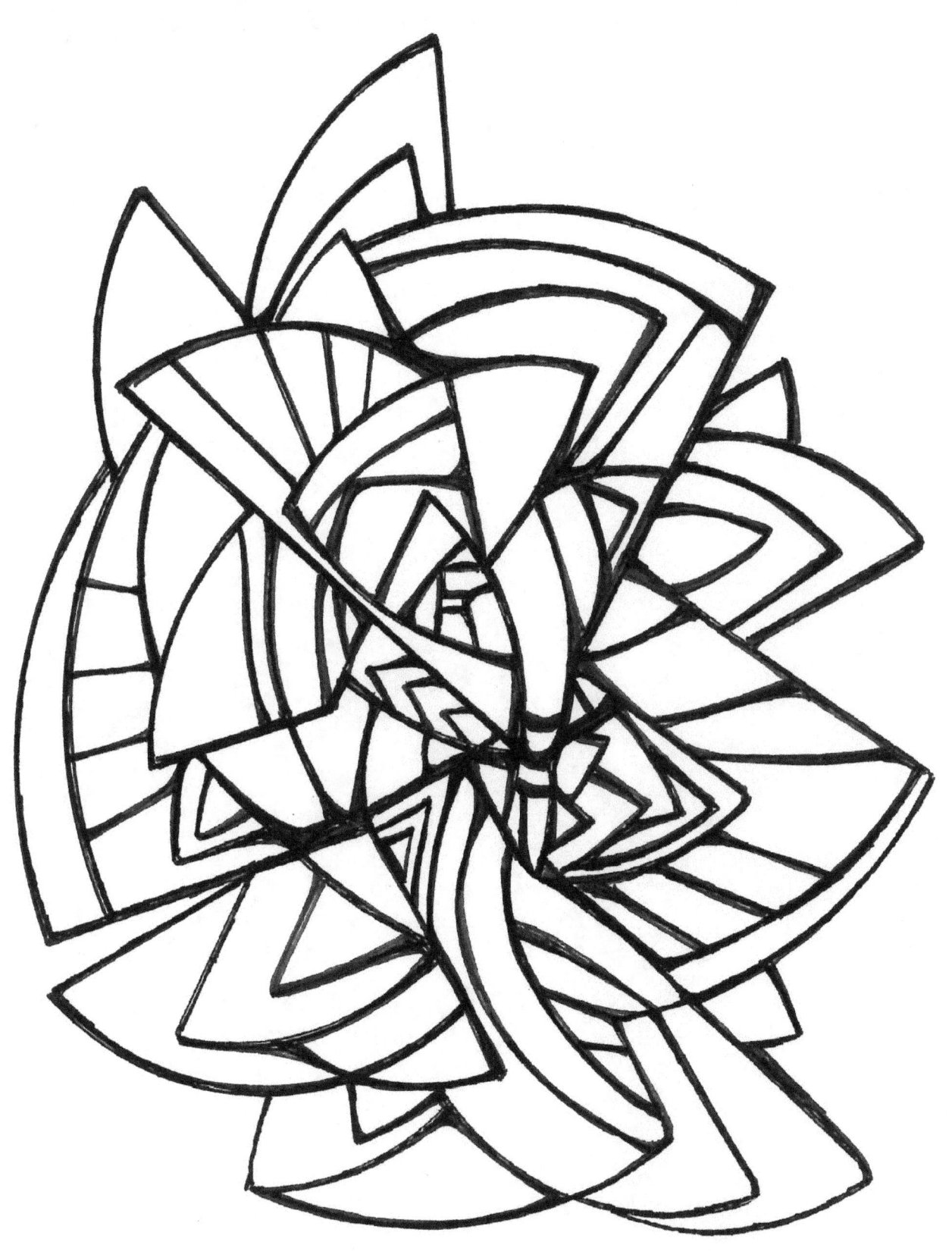

You may wish to place a sheet of paper or poster board under the page you are coloring to prevent damaging the next image.

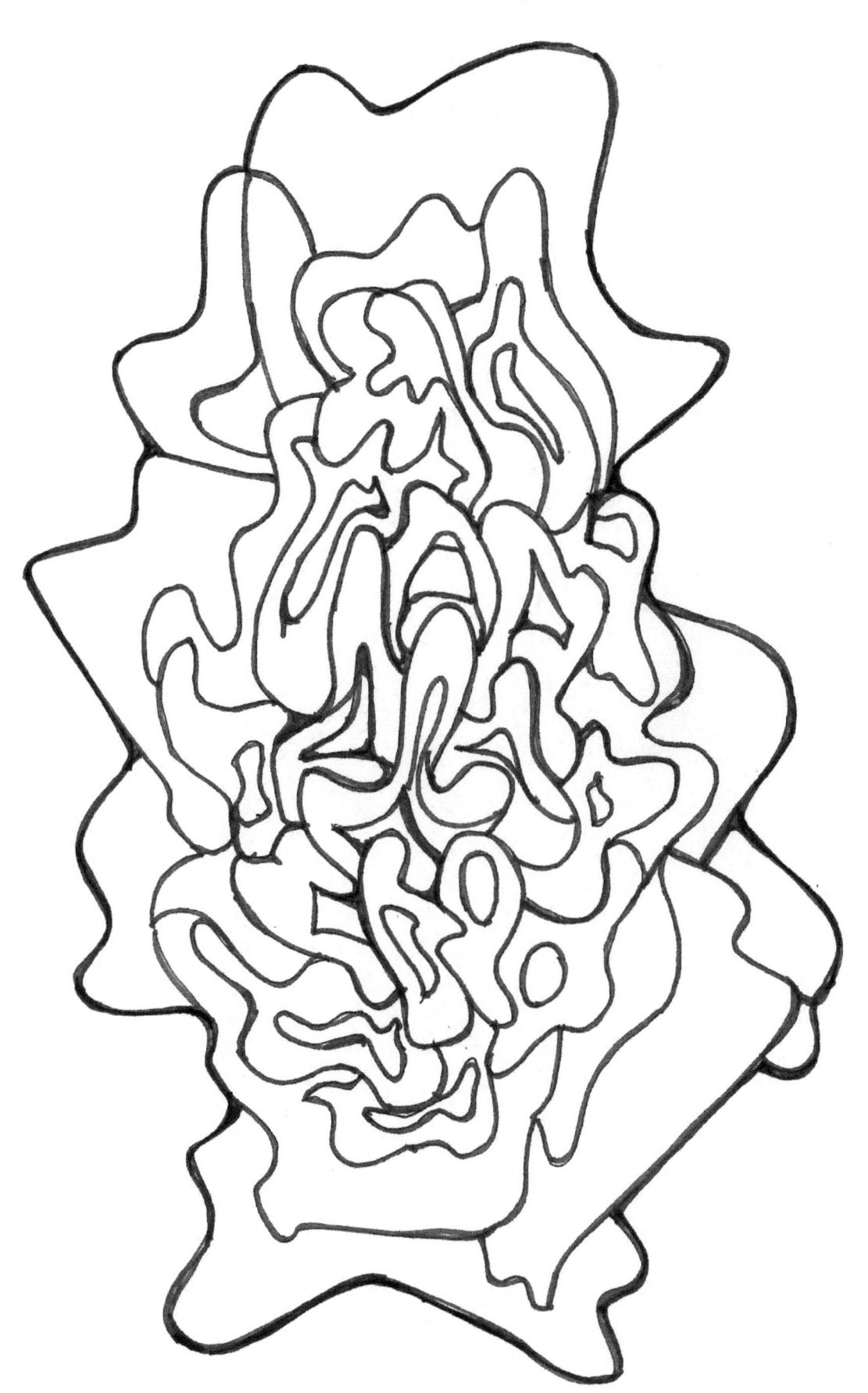

You may wish to place a sheet of paper or poster board under the page you are coloring to prevent damaging the next image.

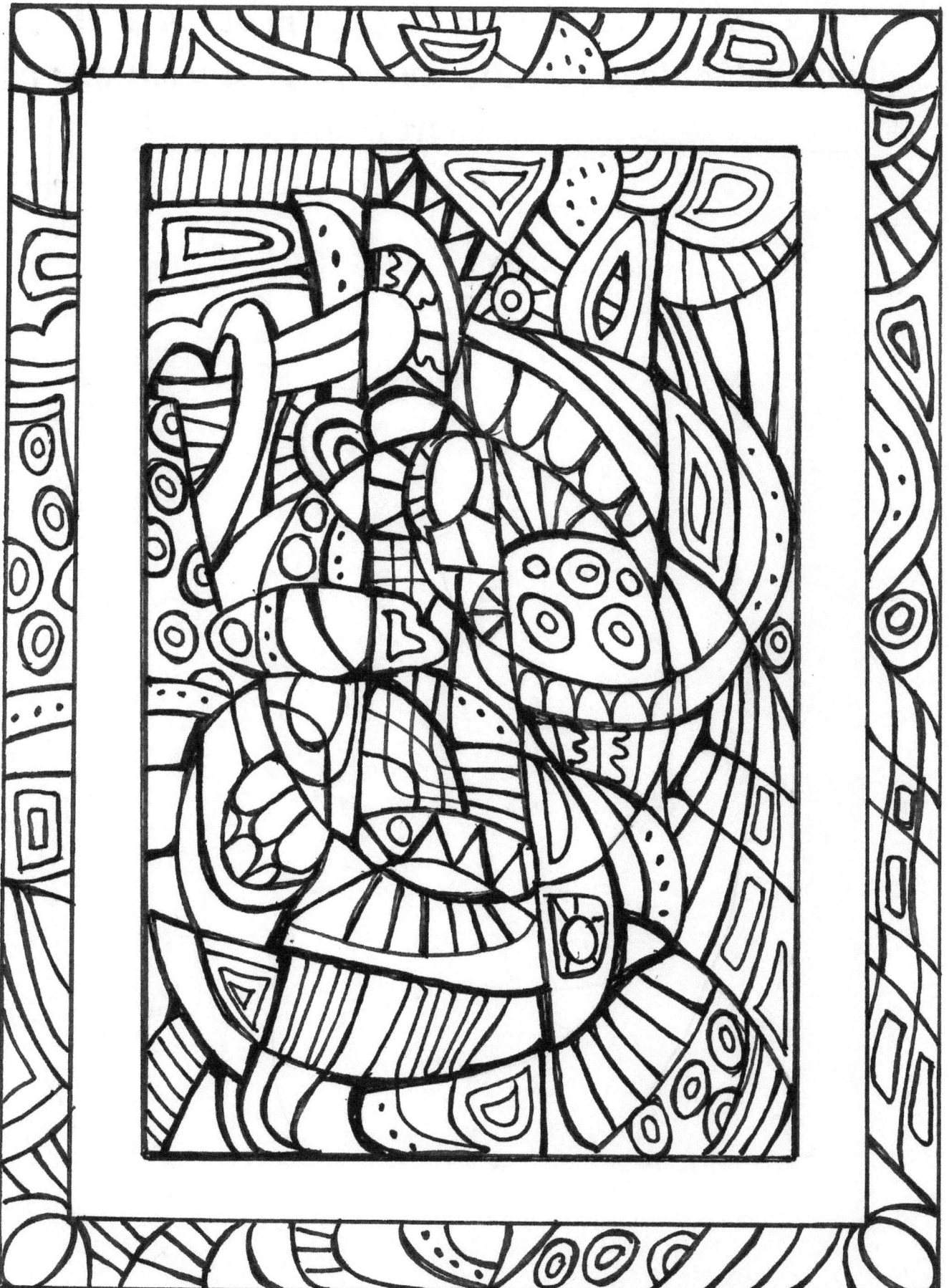

You may wish to place a sheet of paper or poster board under the page you are coloring to prevent damaging the next image.

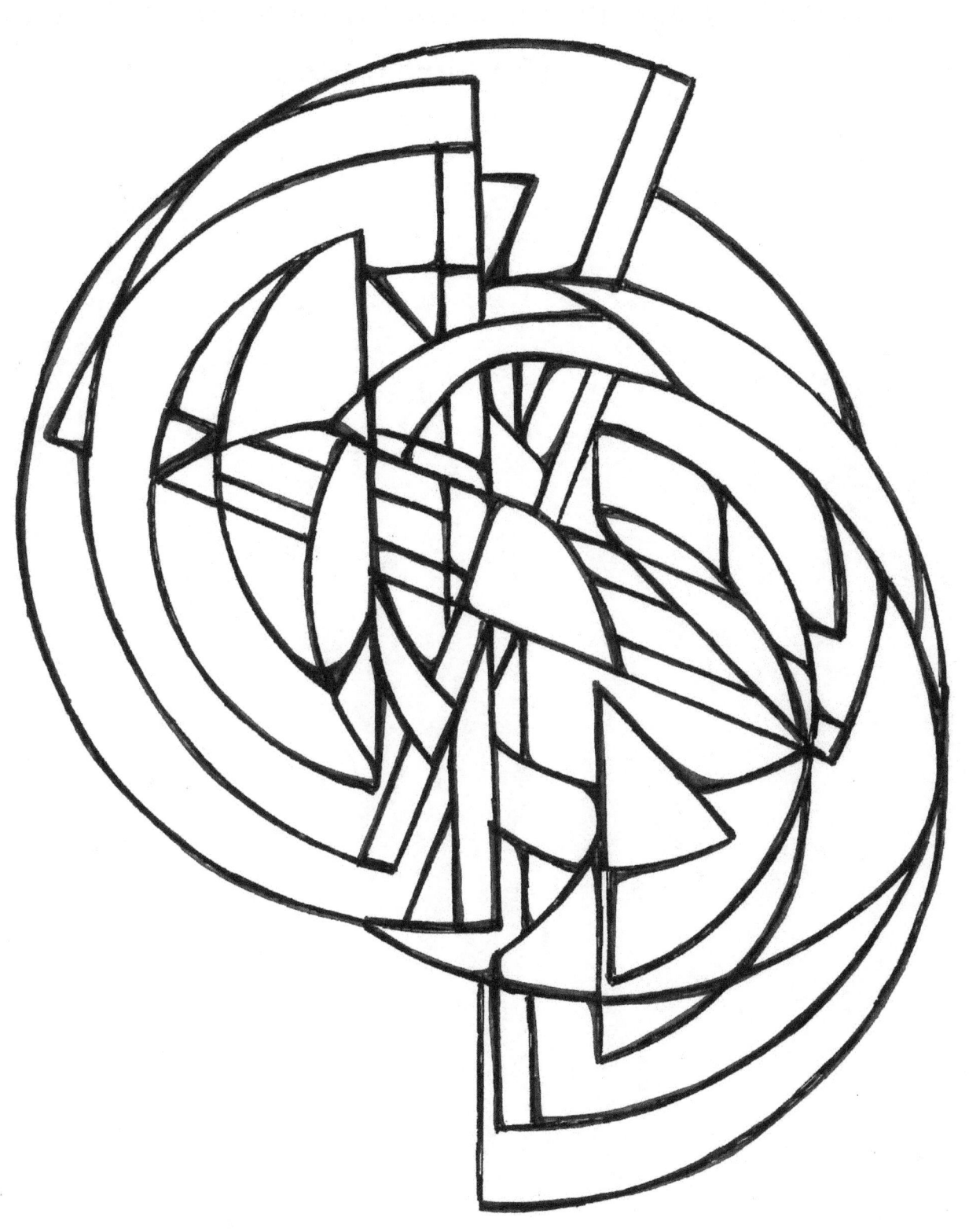

You may wish to place a sheet of paper or poster board under the page you are coloring to prevent damaging the next image.

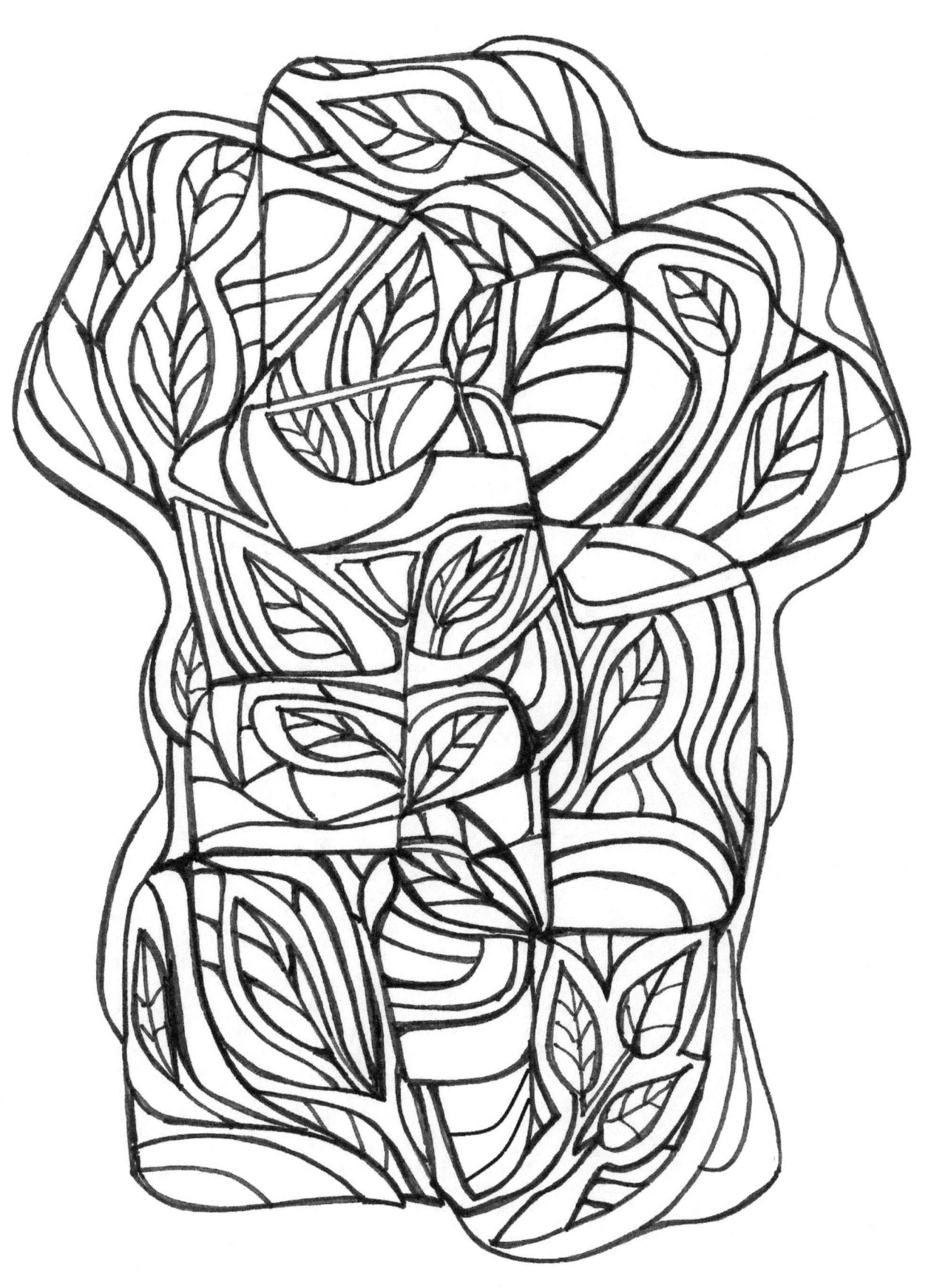

You may wish to place a sheet of paper or poster board under the page you are coloring to prevent damaging the next image.

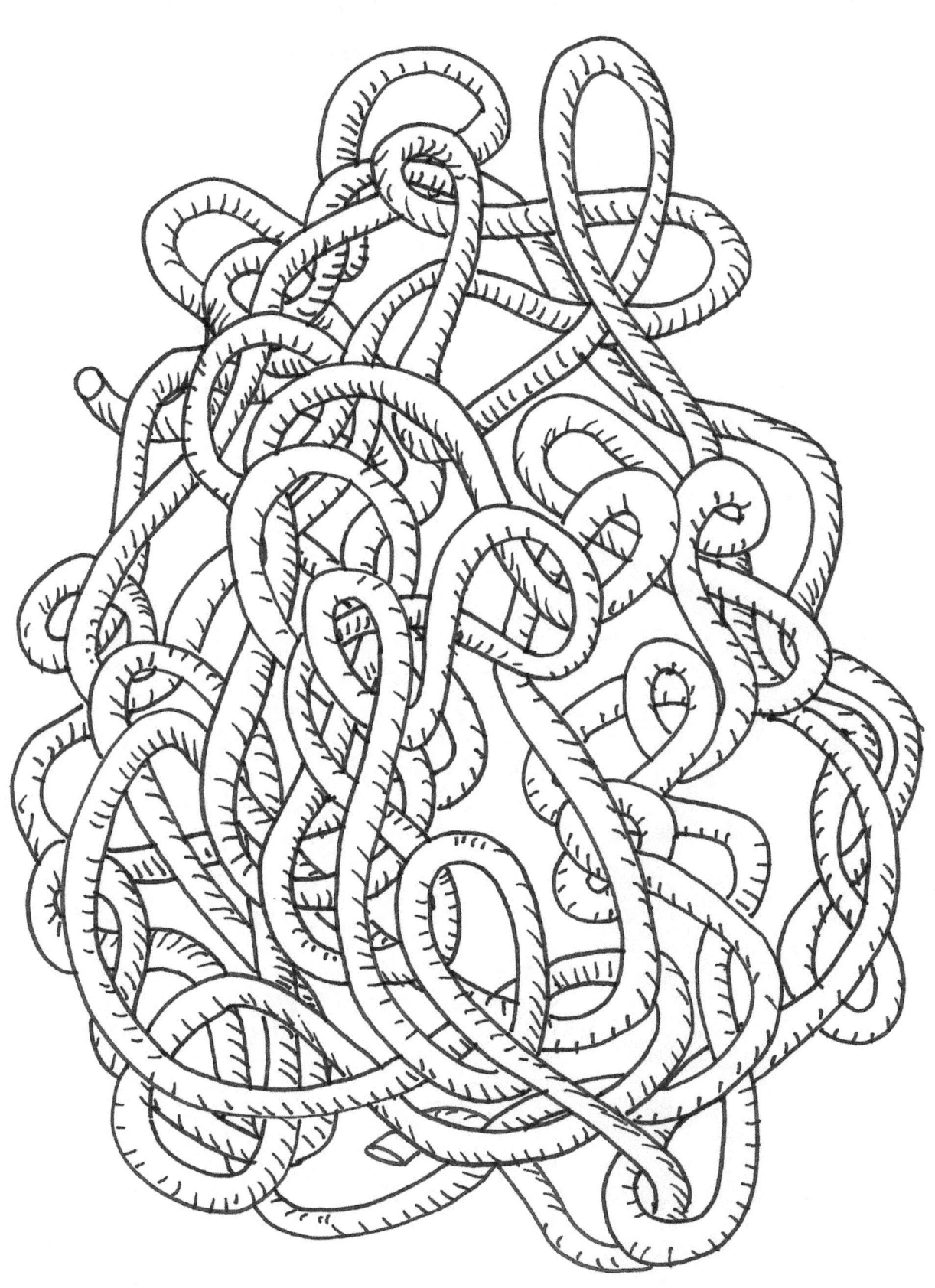

You may wish to place a sheet of paper or poster board under the page you are coloring to prevent damaging the next image.

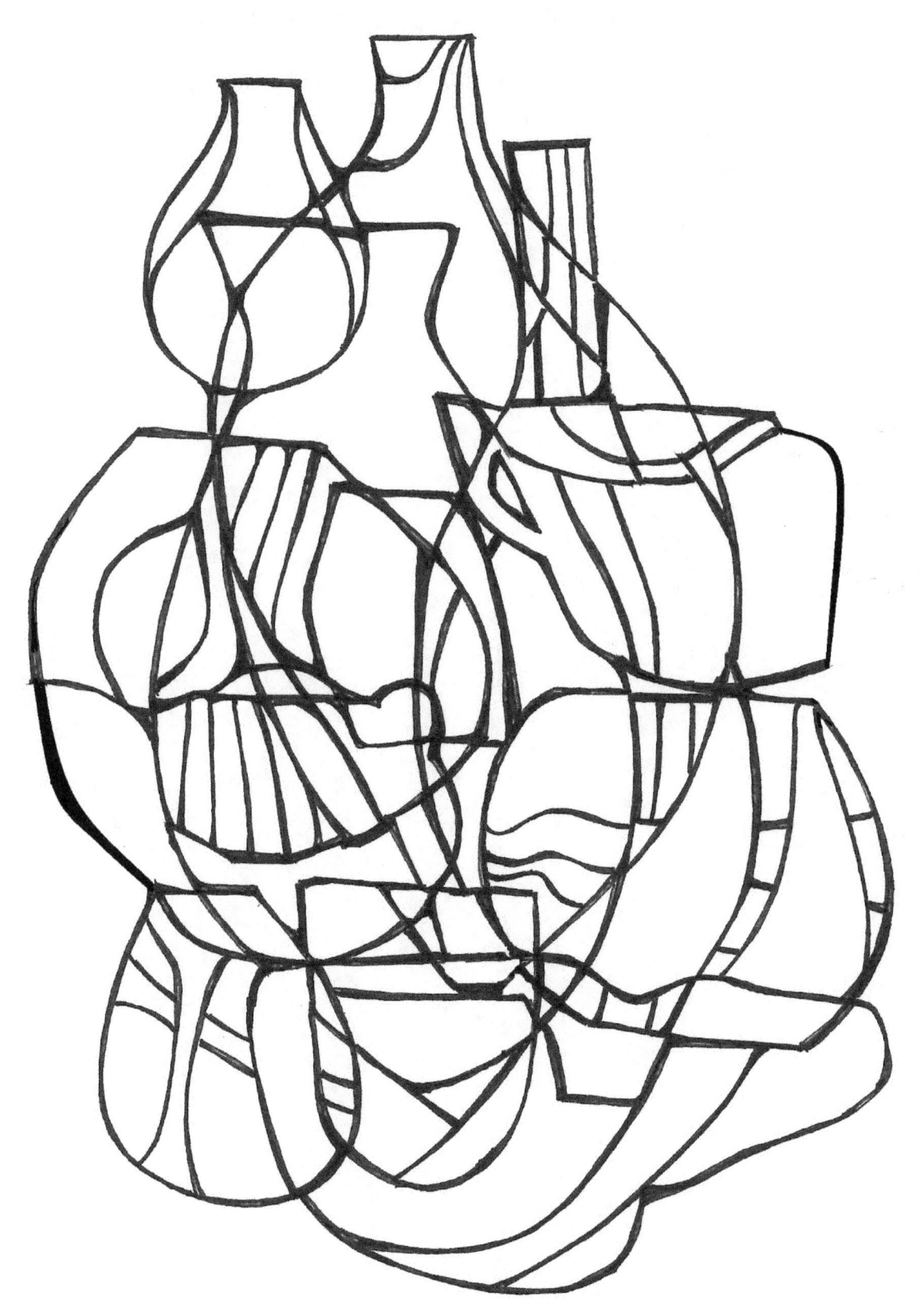

You may wish to place a sheet of paper or poster board under the page you are coloring to prevent damaging the next image.

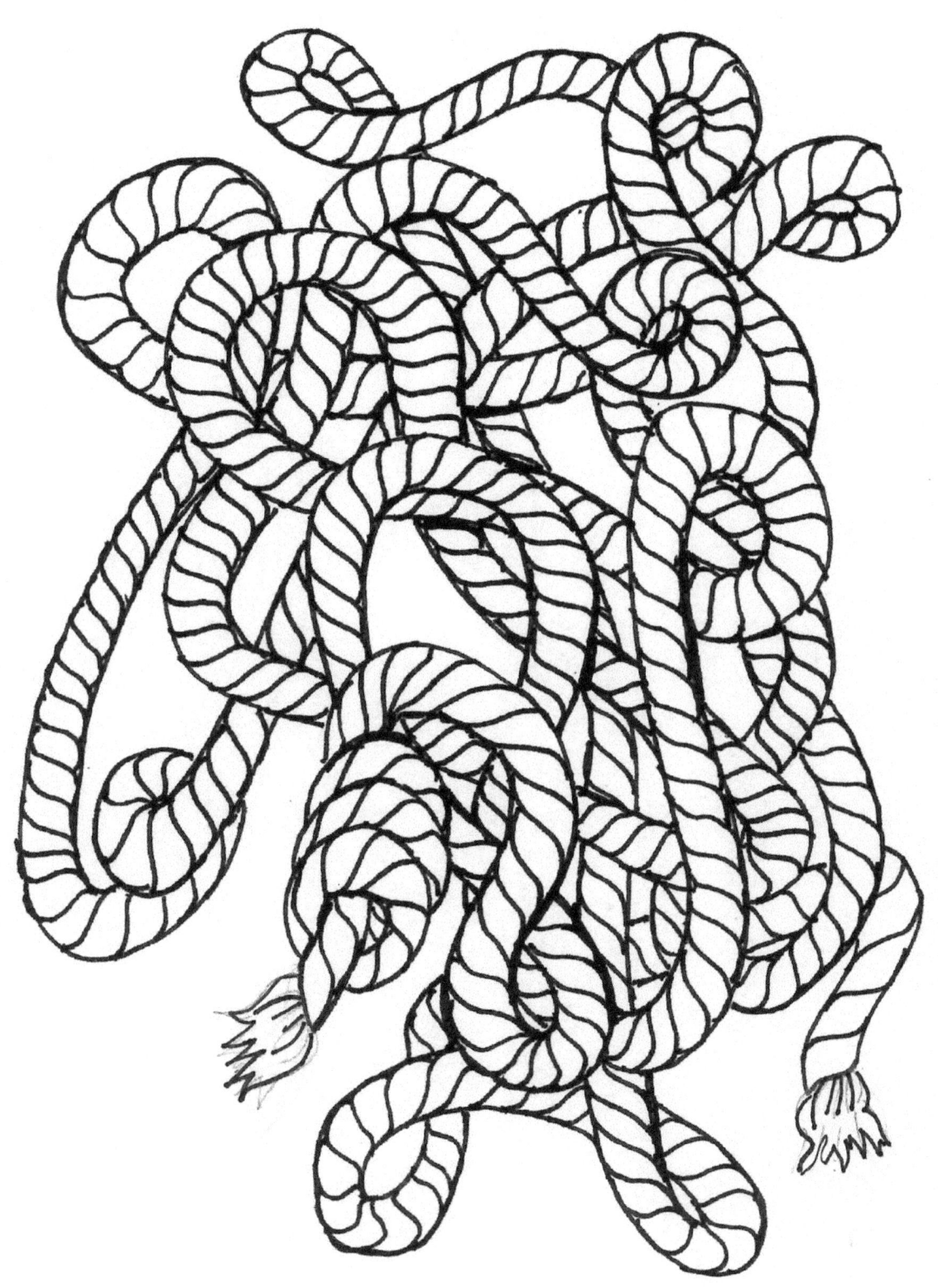

You may wish to place a sheet of paper or poster board under the page you are coloring to prevent damaging the next image.

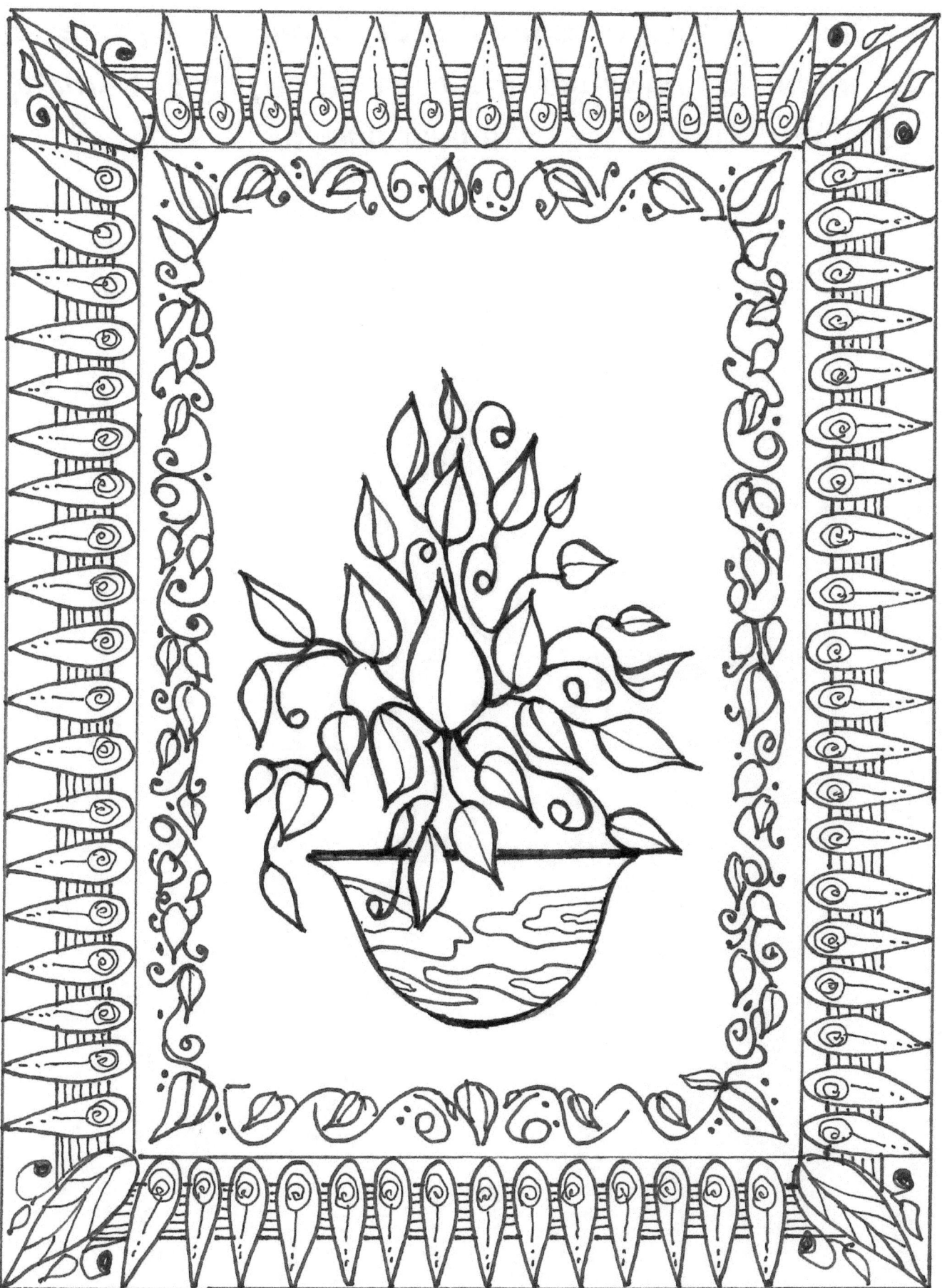

You may wish to place a sheet of paper or poster board under the page you are coloring to prevent damaging the next image.

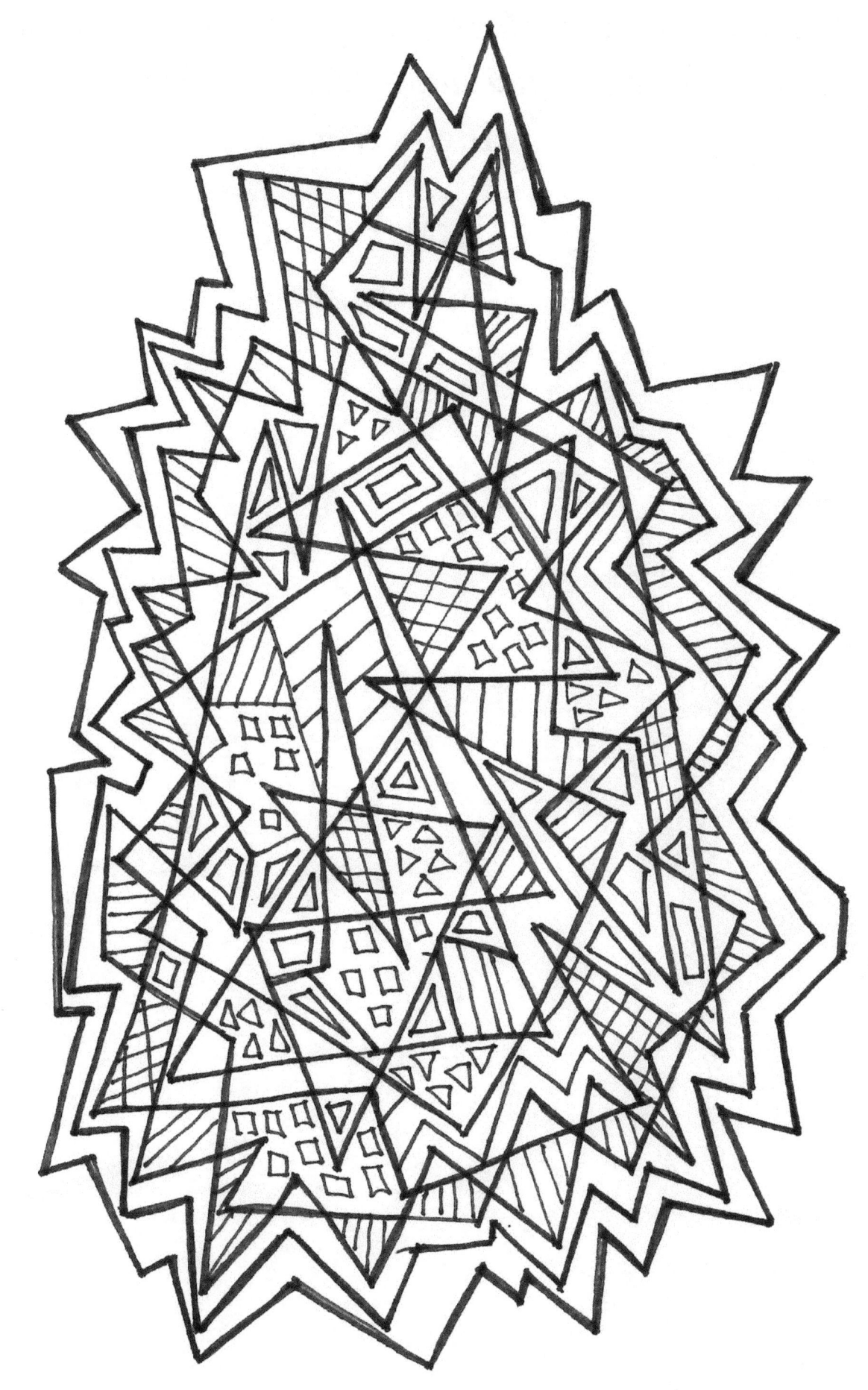

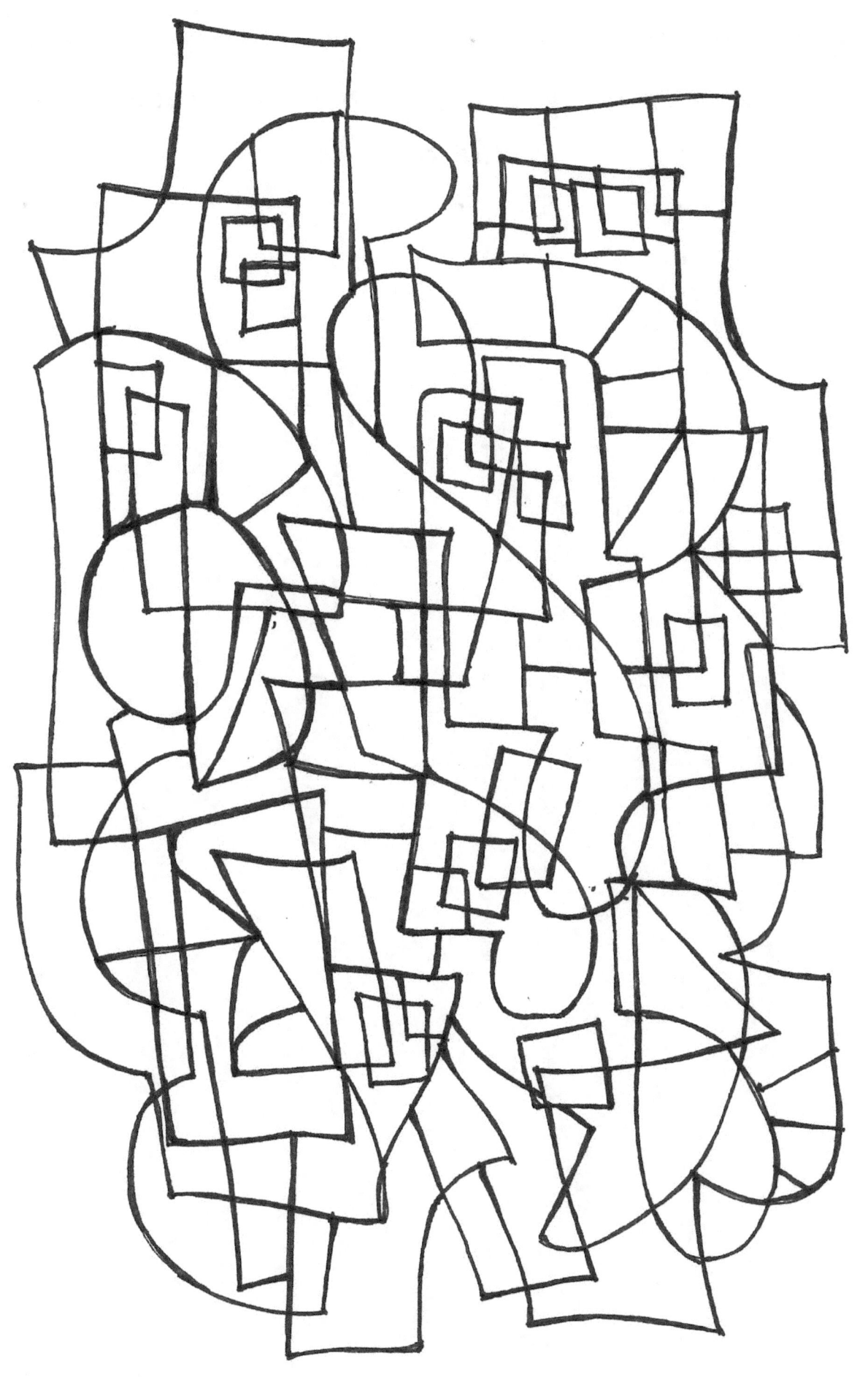

You may wish to place a sheet of paper or poster board under the page you are coloring to prevent damaging the next image.

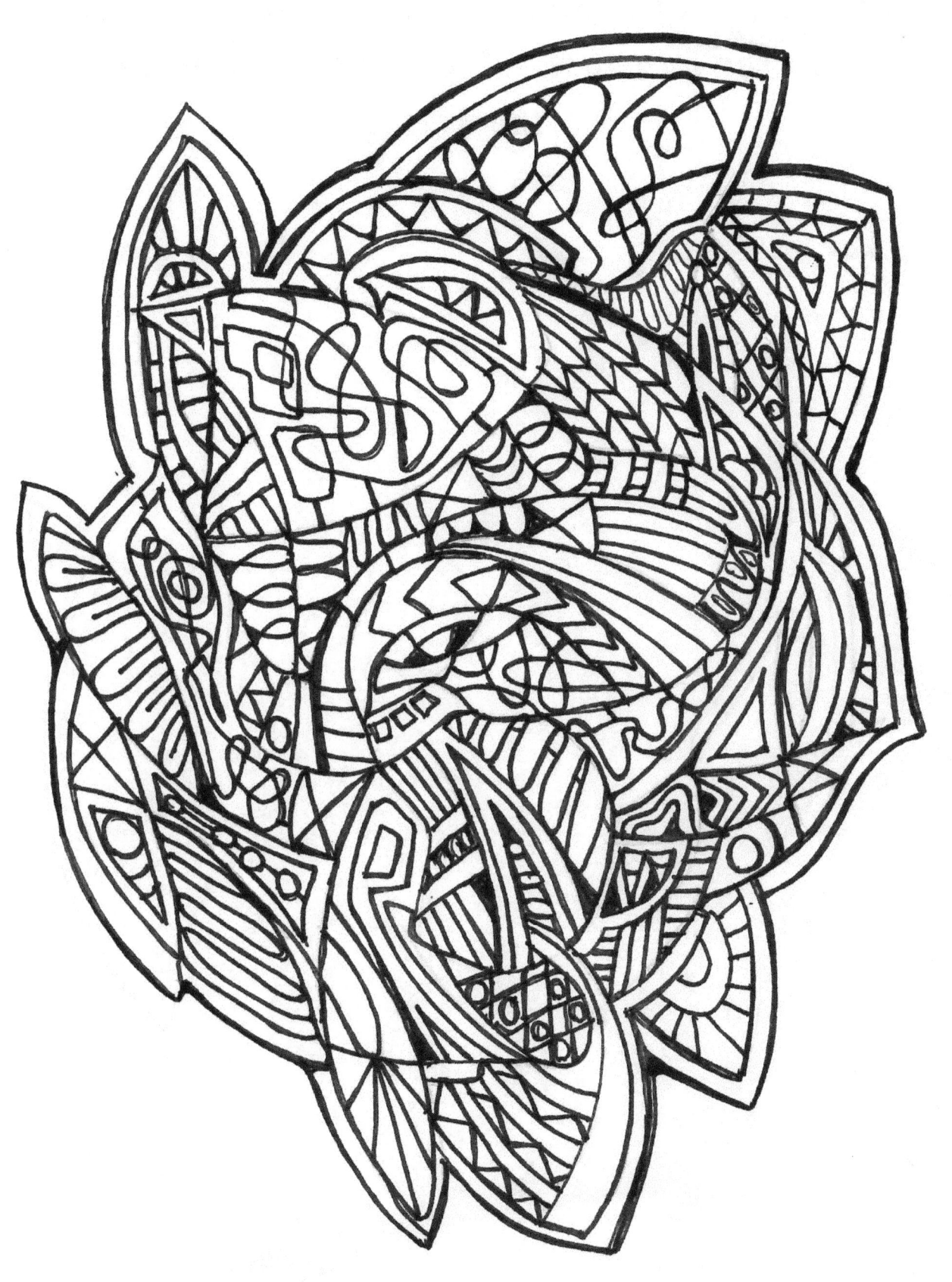

You may wish to place a sheet of paper or poster board under the page you are coloring to prevent damaging the next image.

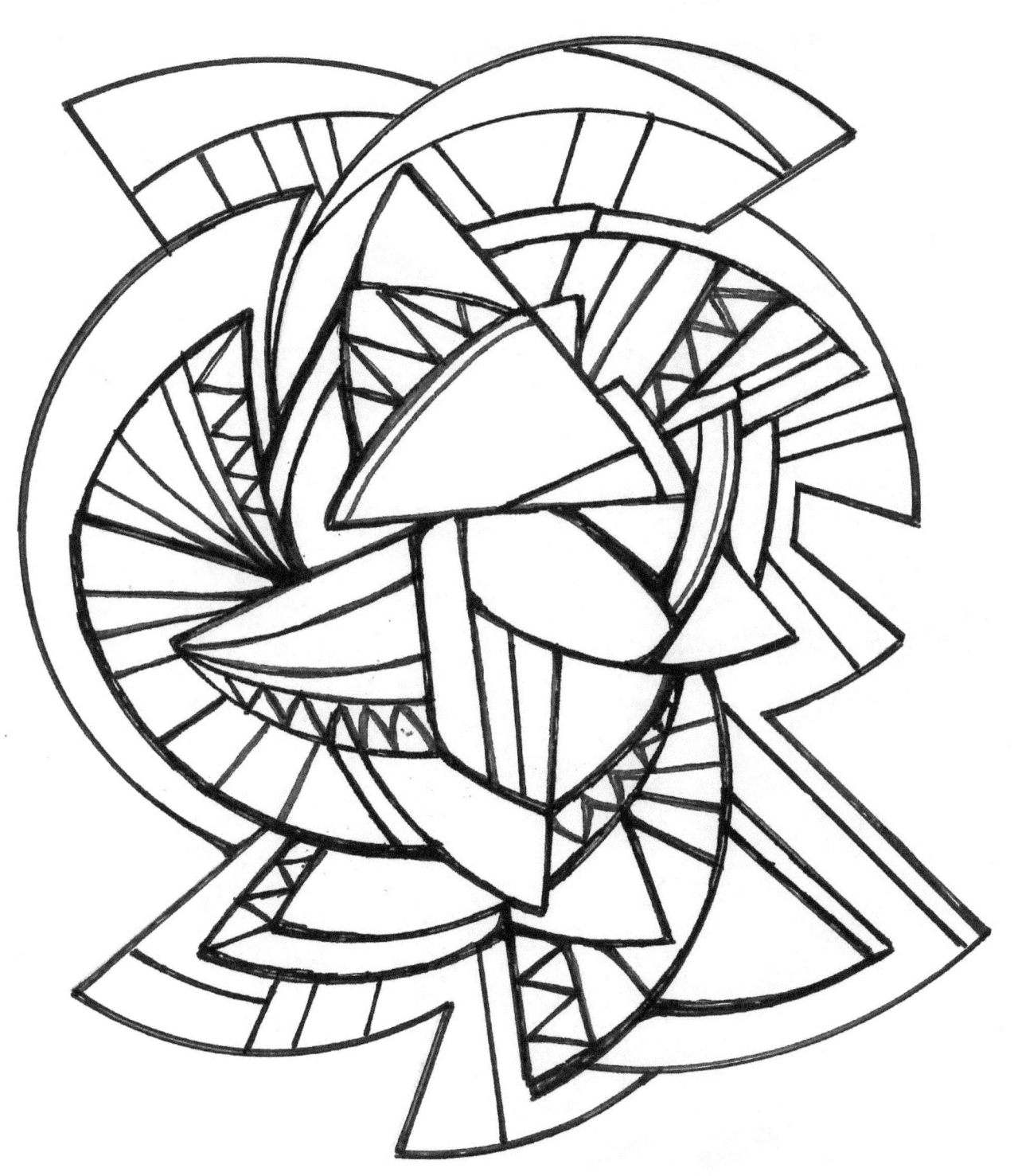

You may wish to place a sheet of paper or poster board under the page you are coloring to prevent damaging the next image.

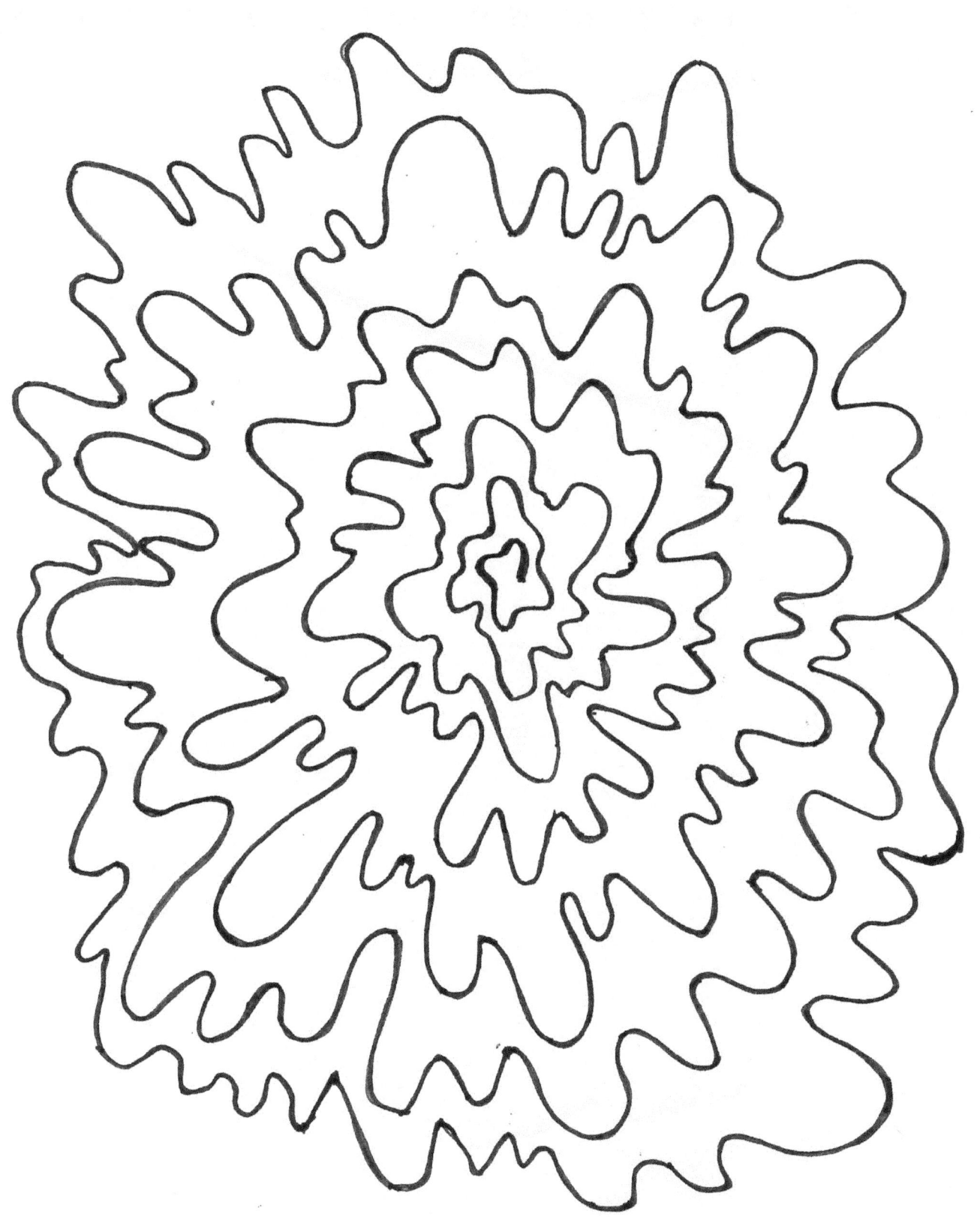

You may wish to place a sheet of paper or poster board under the page you are coloring to prevent damaging the next image.

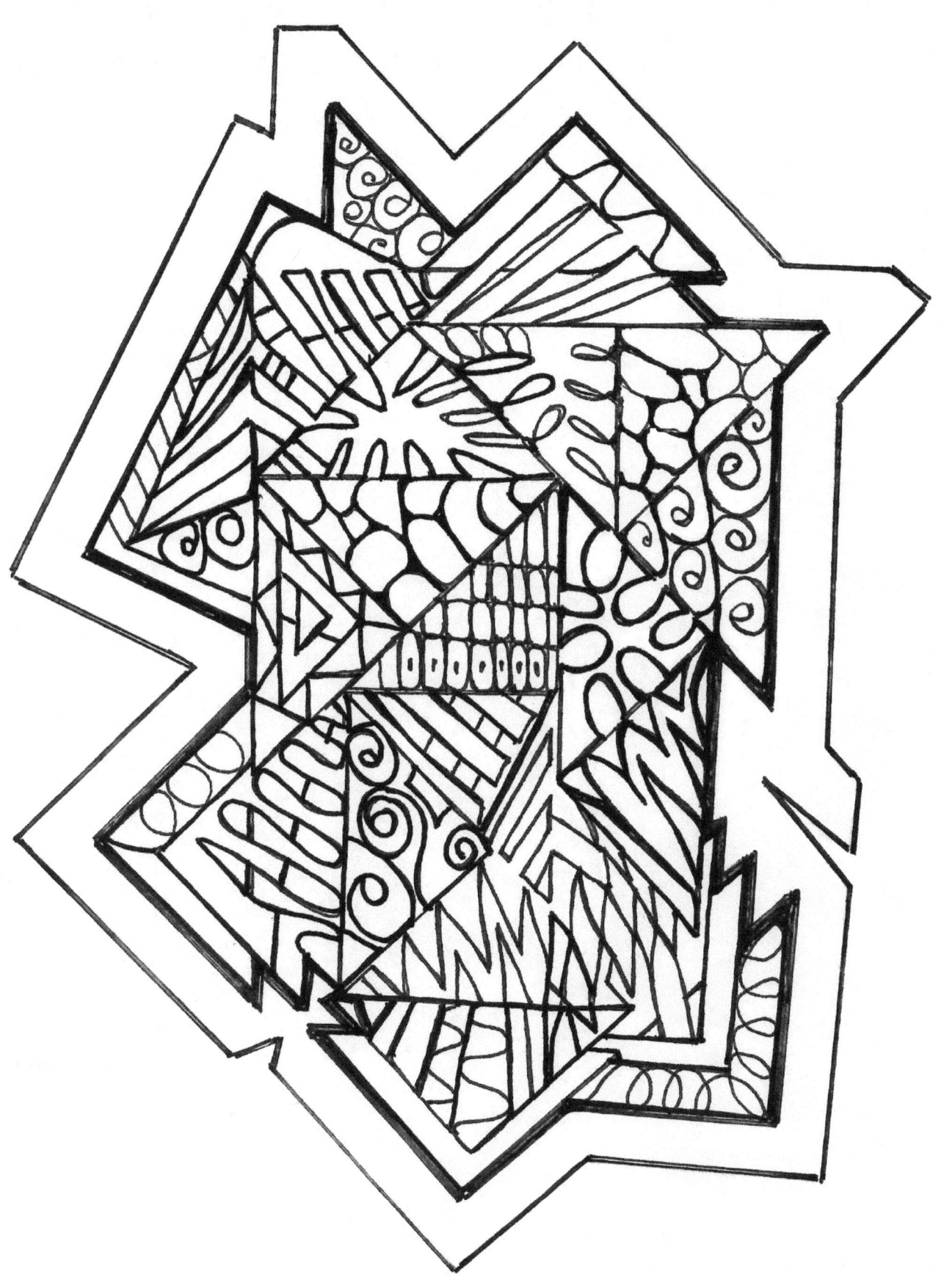

You may wish to place a sheet of paper or poster board under the page you are coloring to prevent damaging the next image.

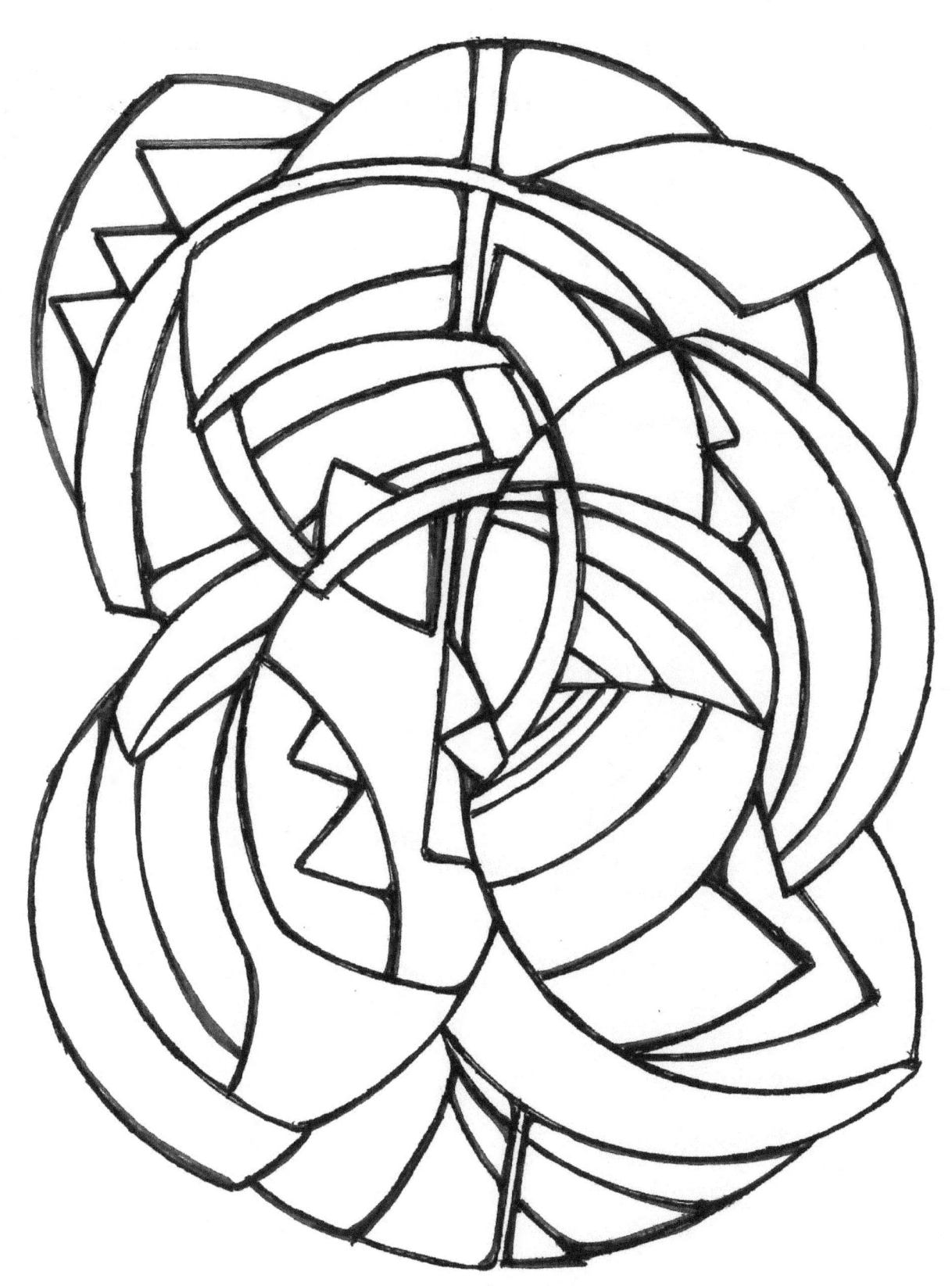

You may wish to place a sheet of paper or poster board under the page you are coloring to prevent damaging the next image.

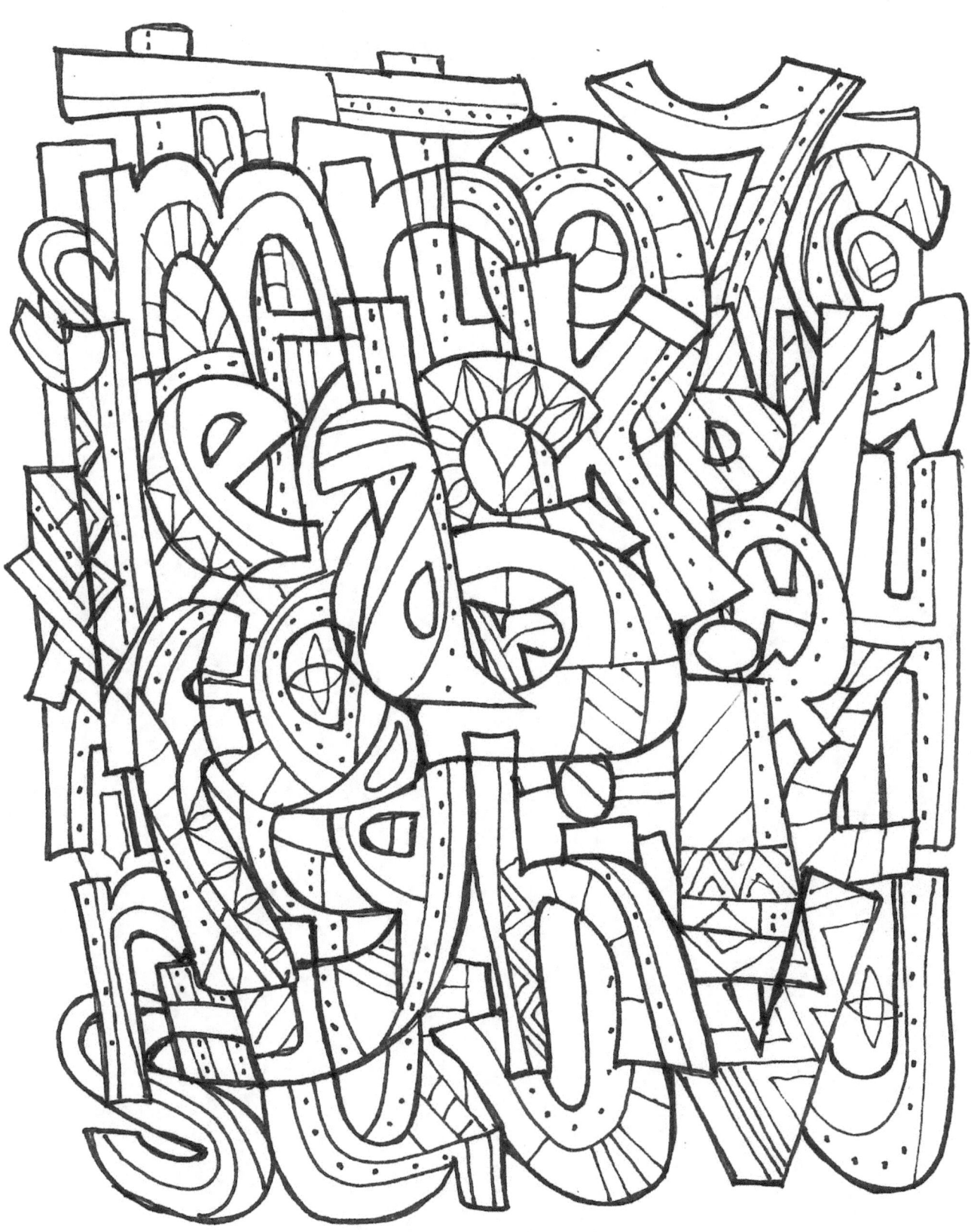

You may wish to place a sheet of paper or poster board under the page you are coloring to prevent damaging the next image.

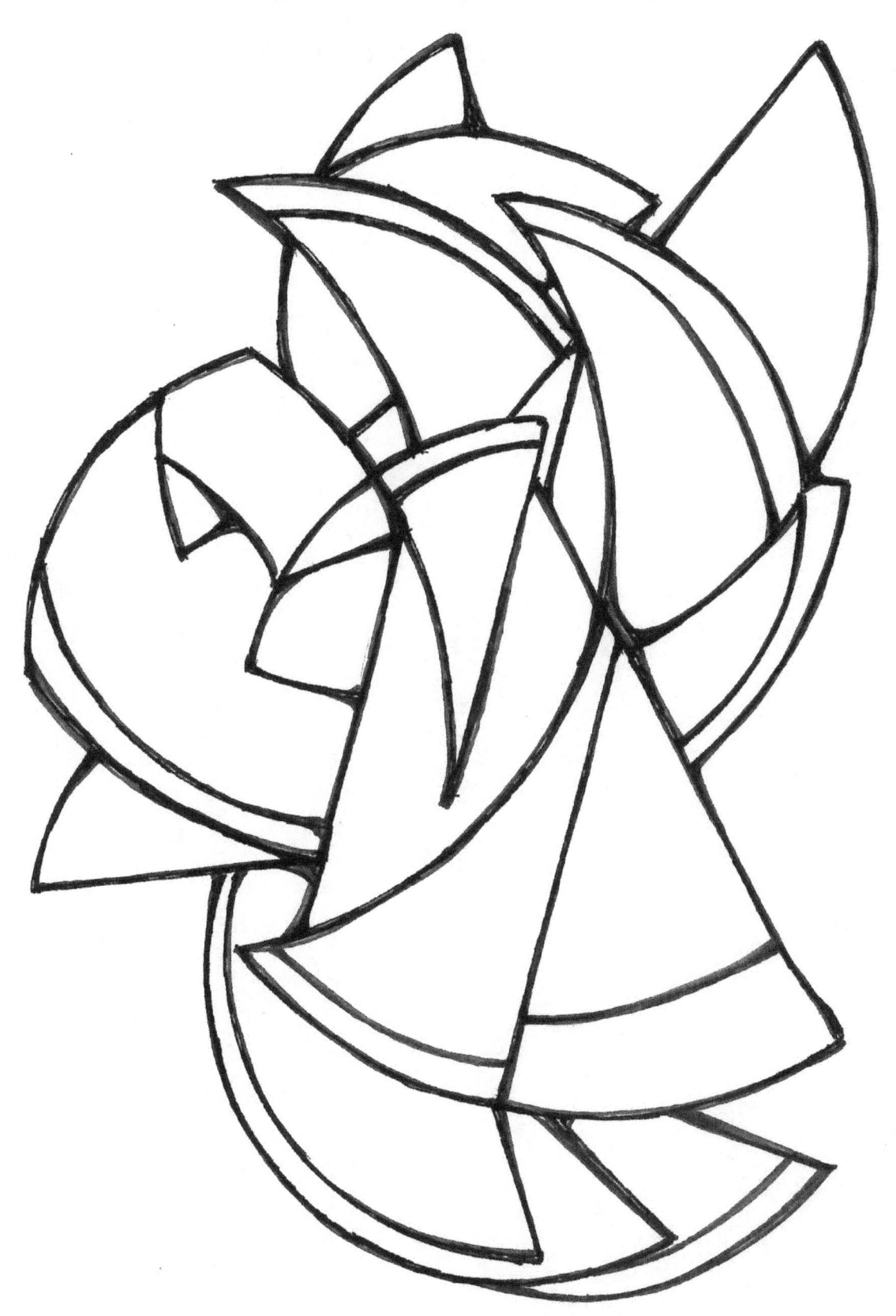

You may wish to place a sheet of paper or poster board under the page you are coloring to prevent damaging the next image.

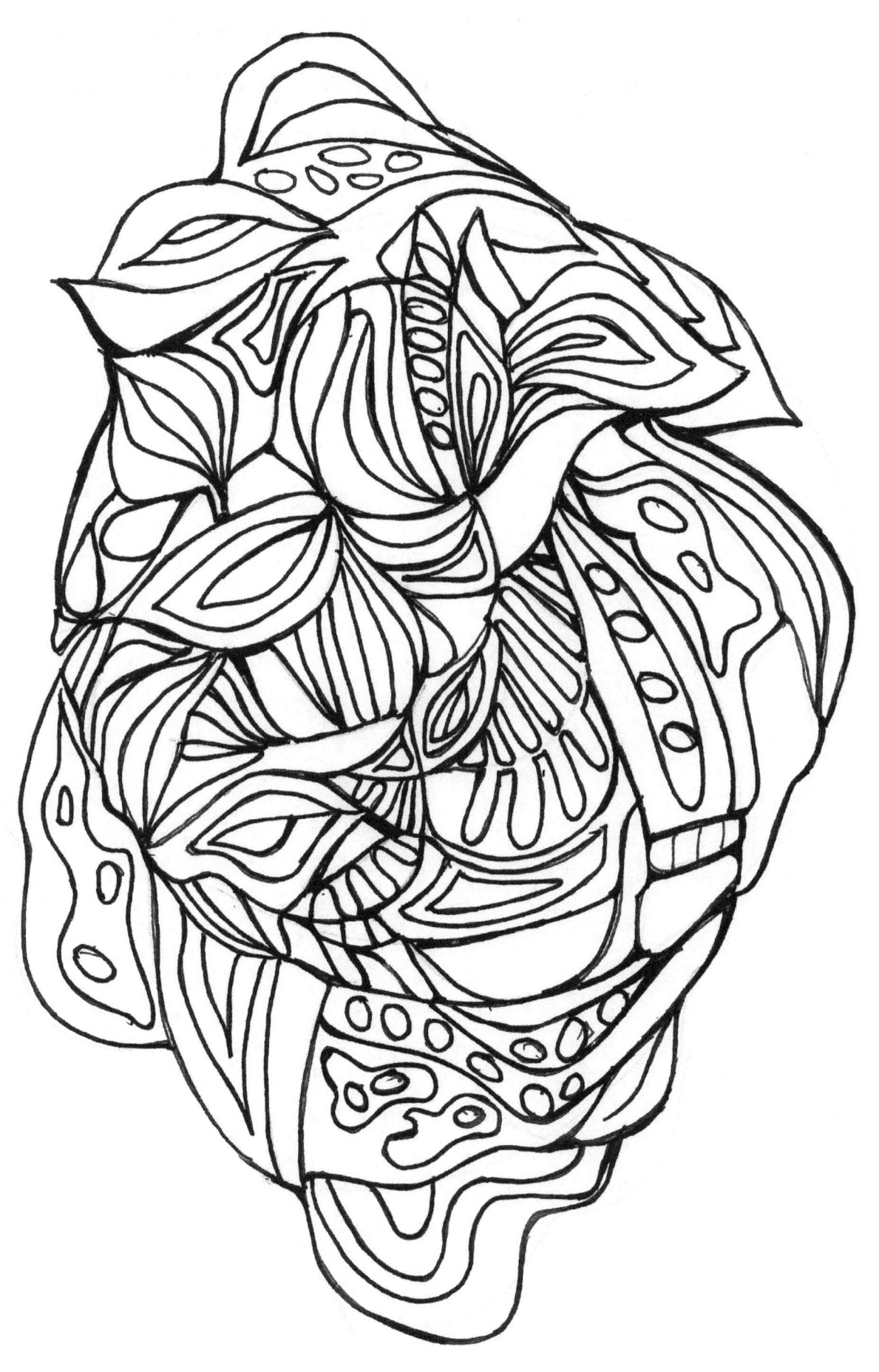

You may wish to place a sheet of paper or poster board under the page you are coloring to prevent damaging the next image.

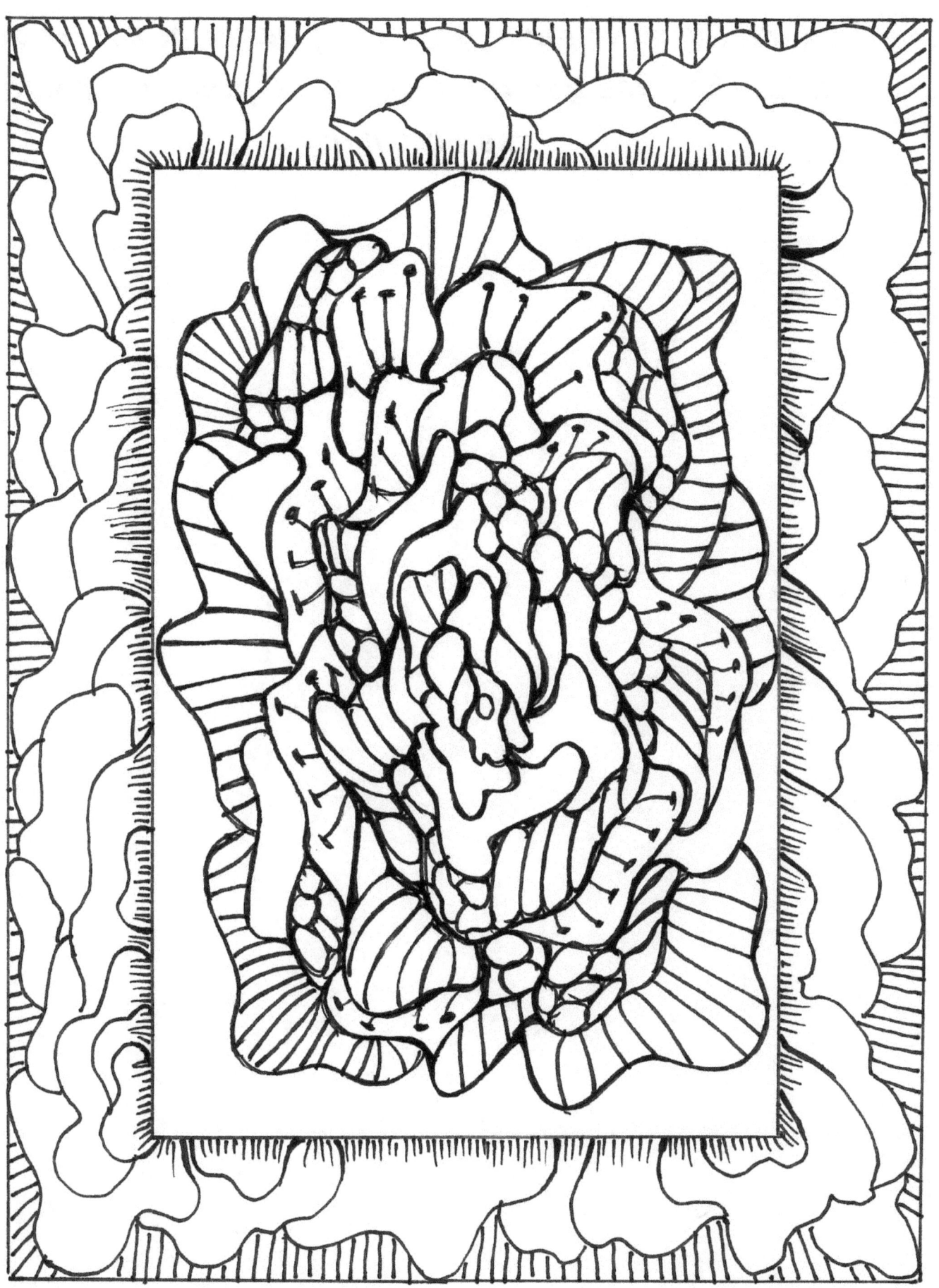

You may wish to place a sheet of paper or poster board under the page you are coloring to prevent damaging the next image.

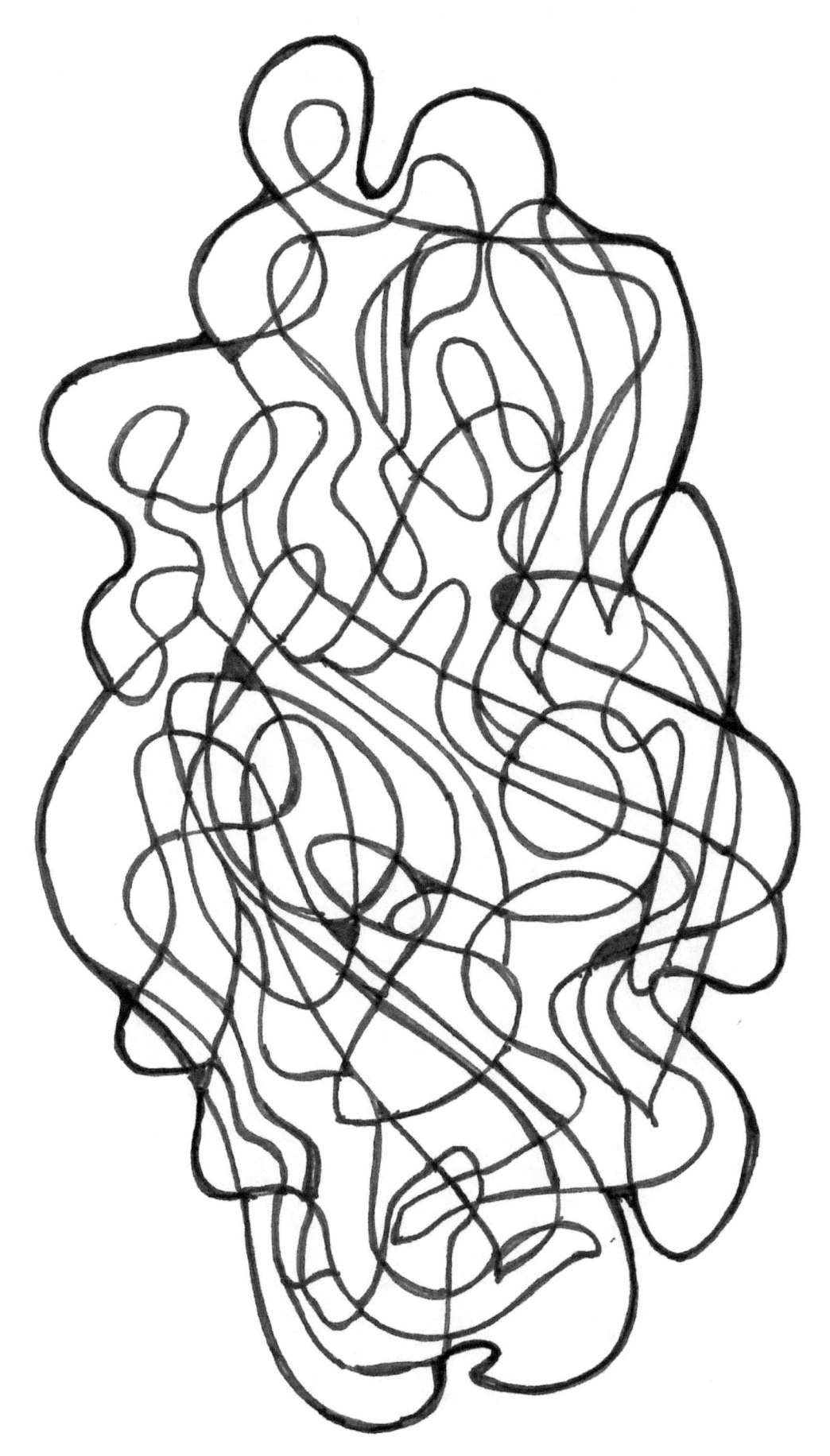

You may wish to place a sheet of paper or poster board under the page you are coloring to prevent damaging the next image.

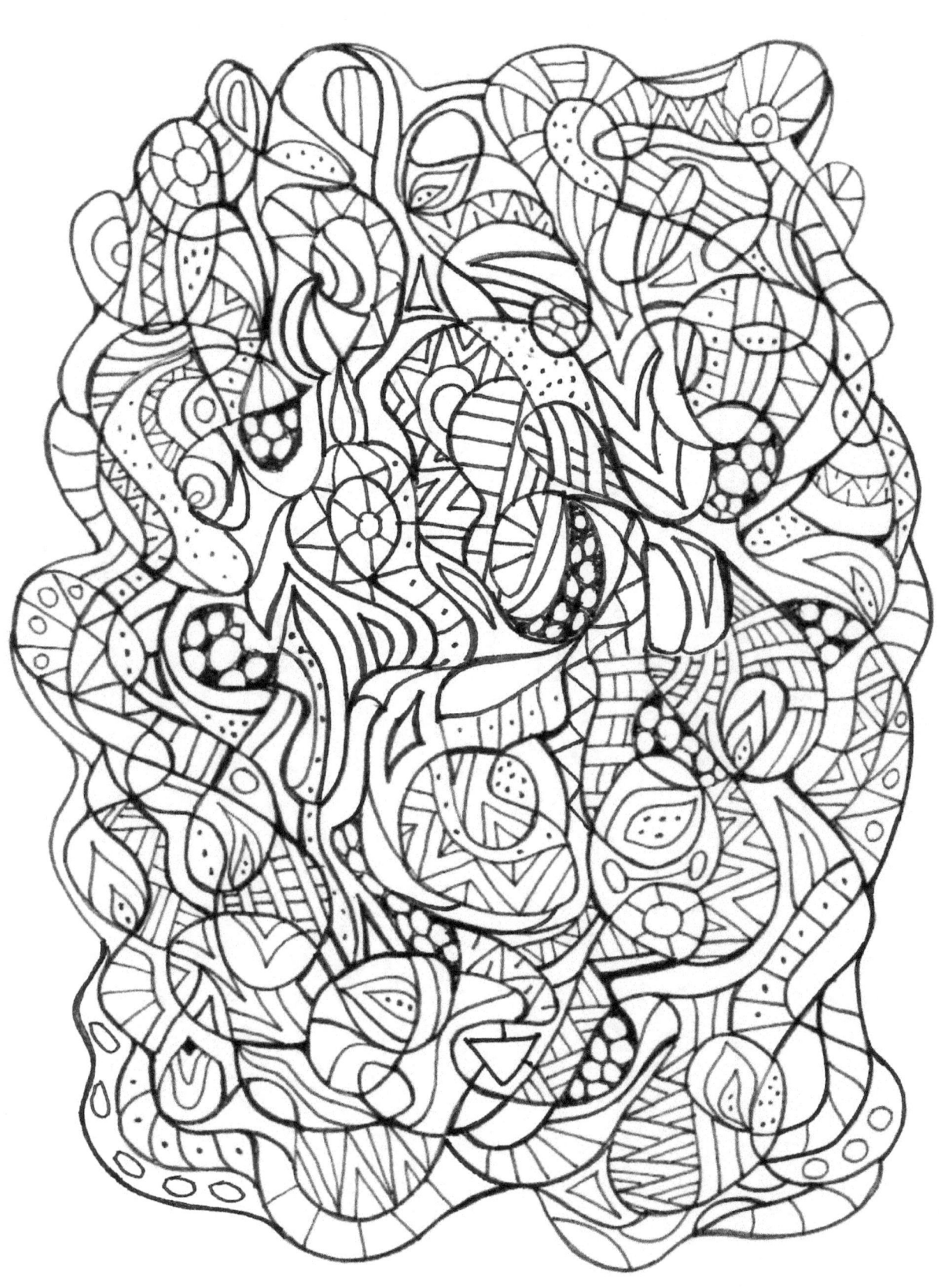

You may wish to place a sheet of paper or poster board under the page you are coloring to prevent damaging the next image.

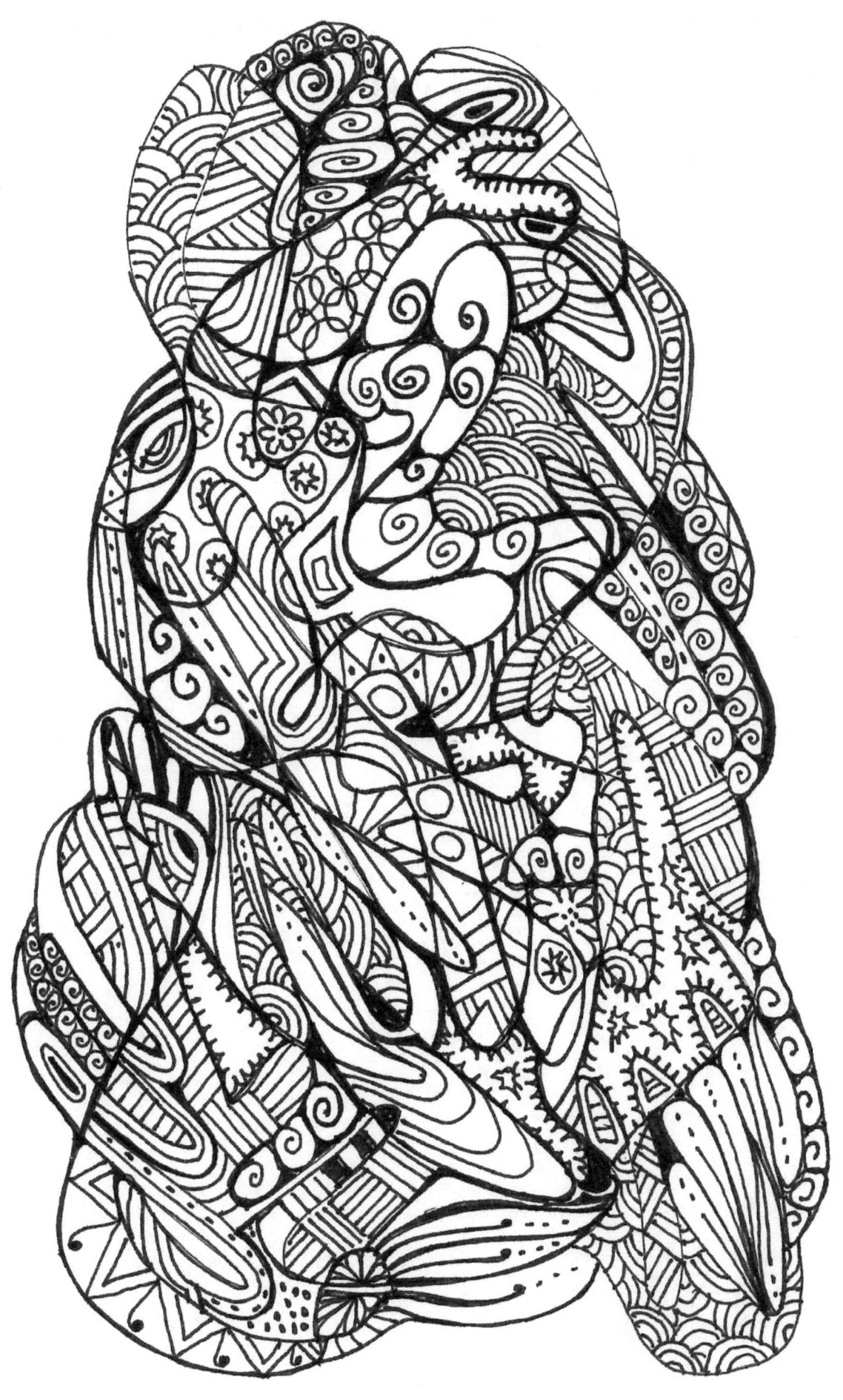

You may wish to place a sheet of paper or poster board under the page you are coloring to prevent damaging the next image.

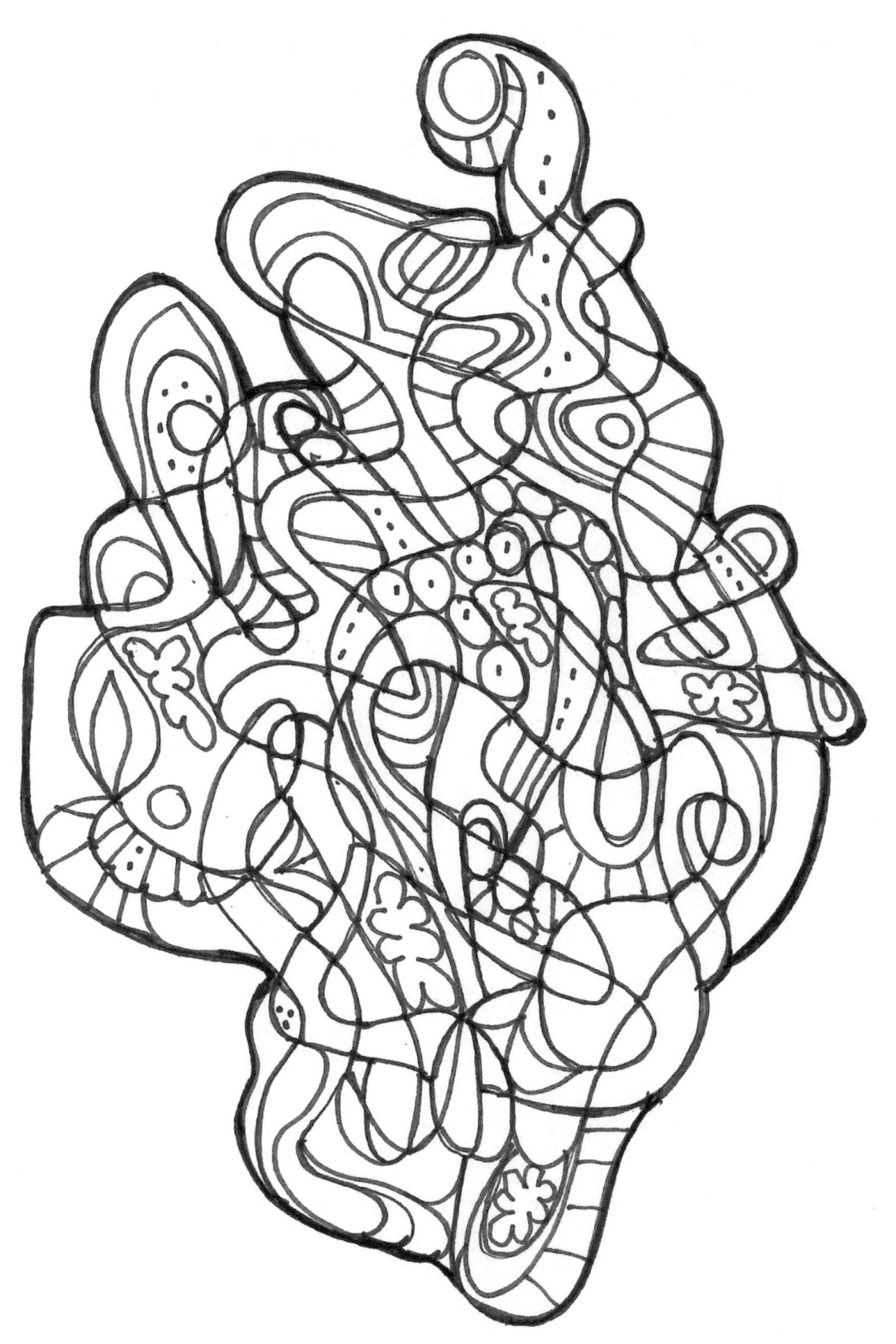

You may wish to place a sheet of paper or poster board under the page you are coloring to prevent damaging the next image.

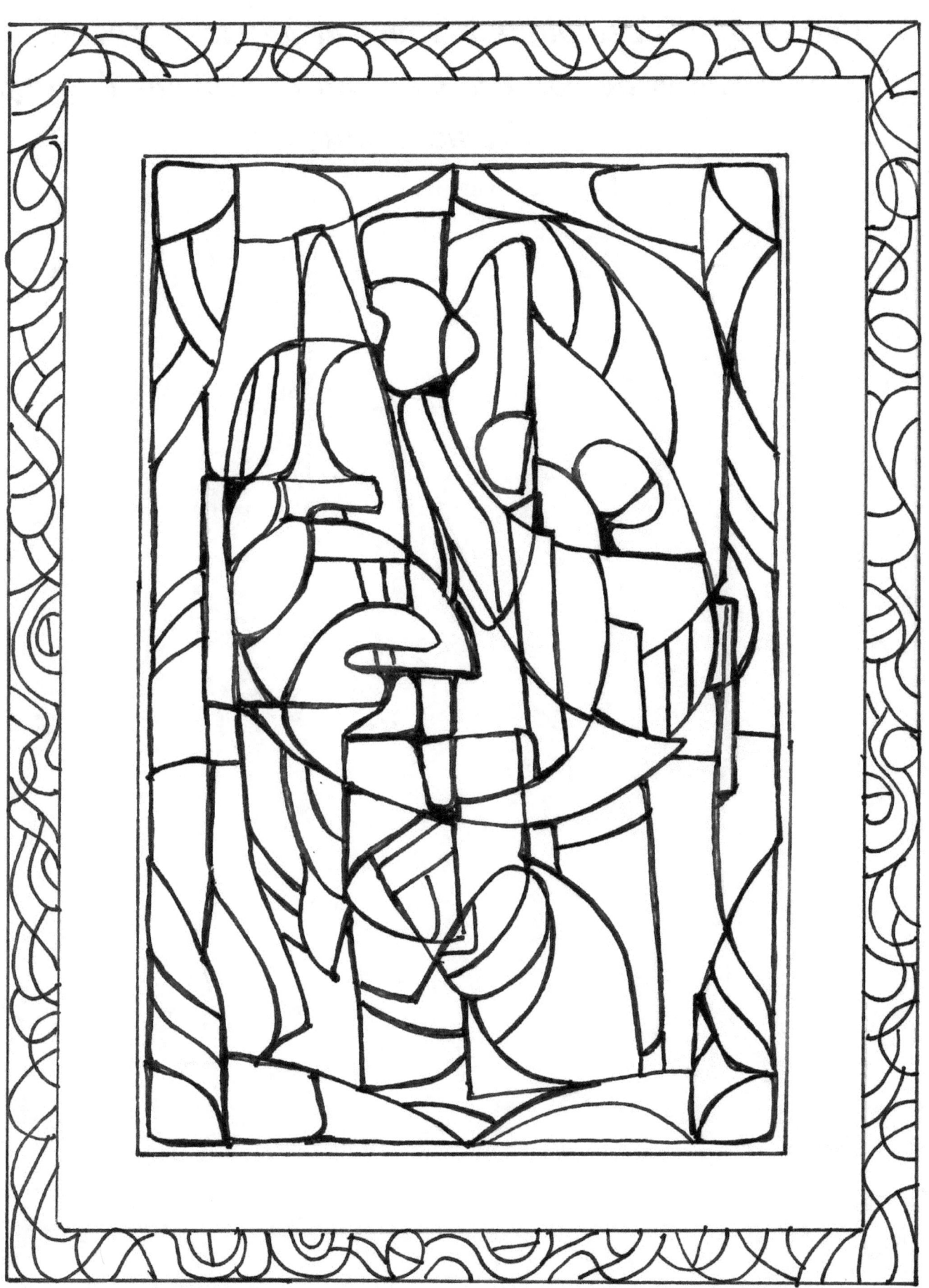

You may wish to place a sheet of paper or poster board under the page you are coloring to prevent damaging the next image.

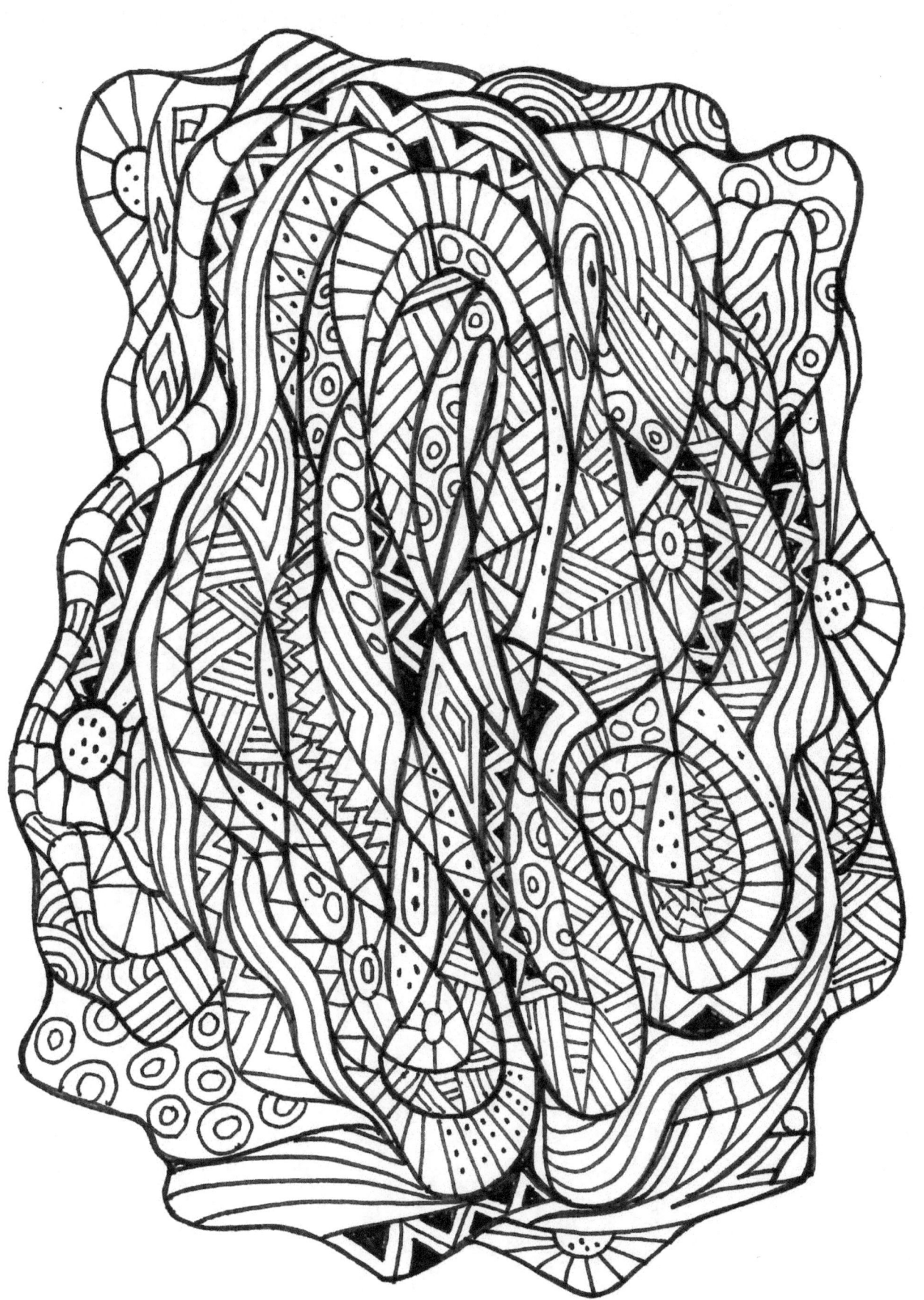

You may wish to place a sheet of paper or poster board under the page you are coloring to prevent damaging the next image.

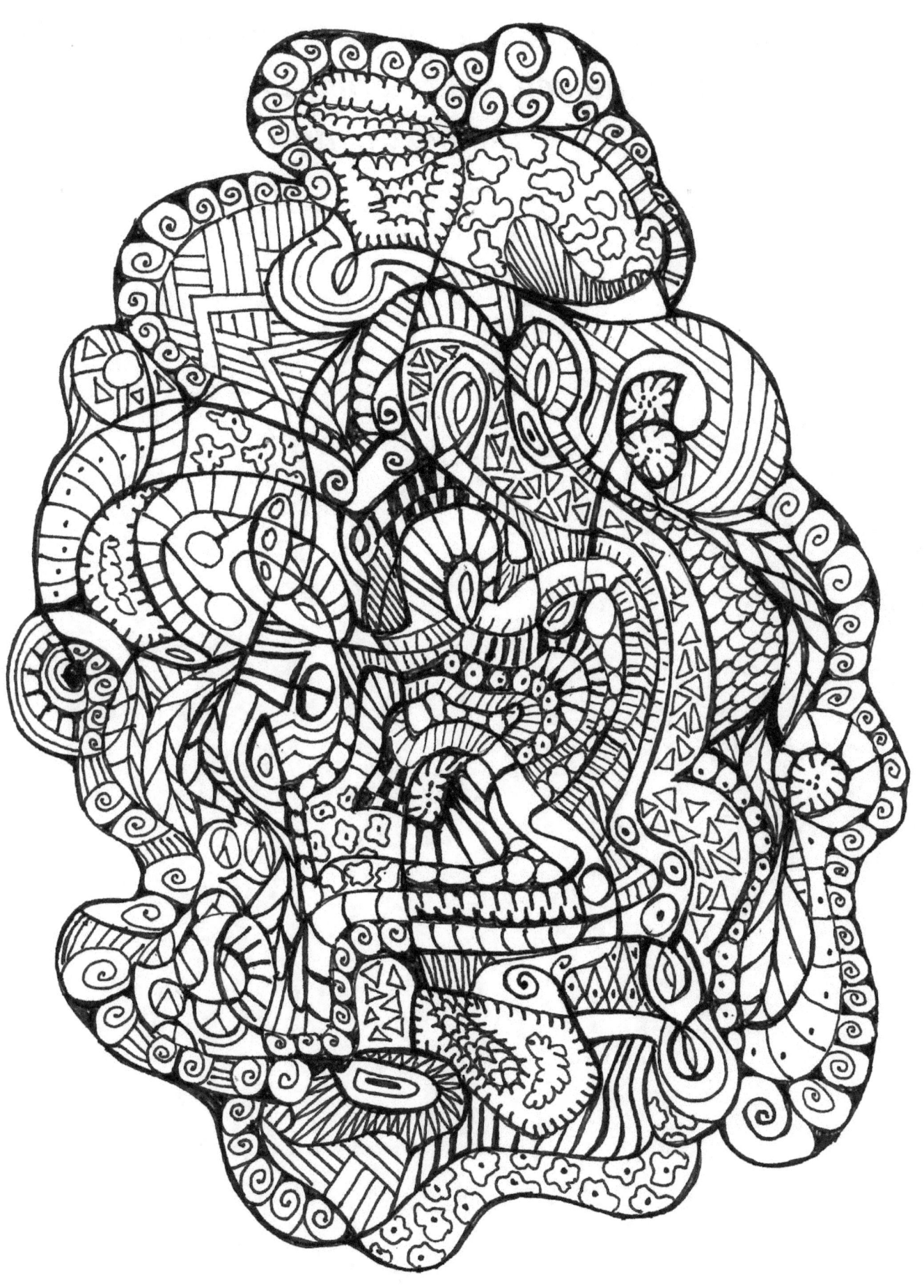

You may wish to place a sheet of paper or poster board under the page you are coloring to prevent damaging the next image.

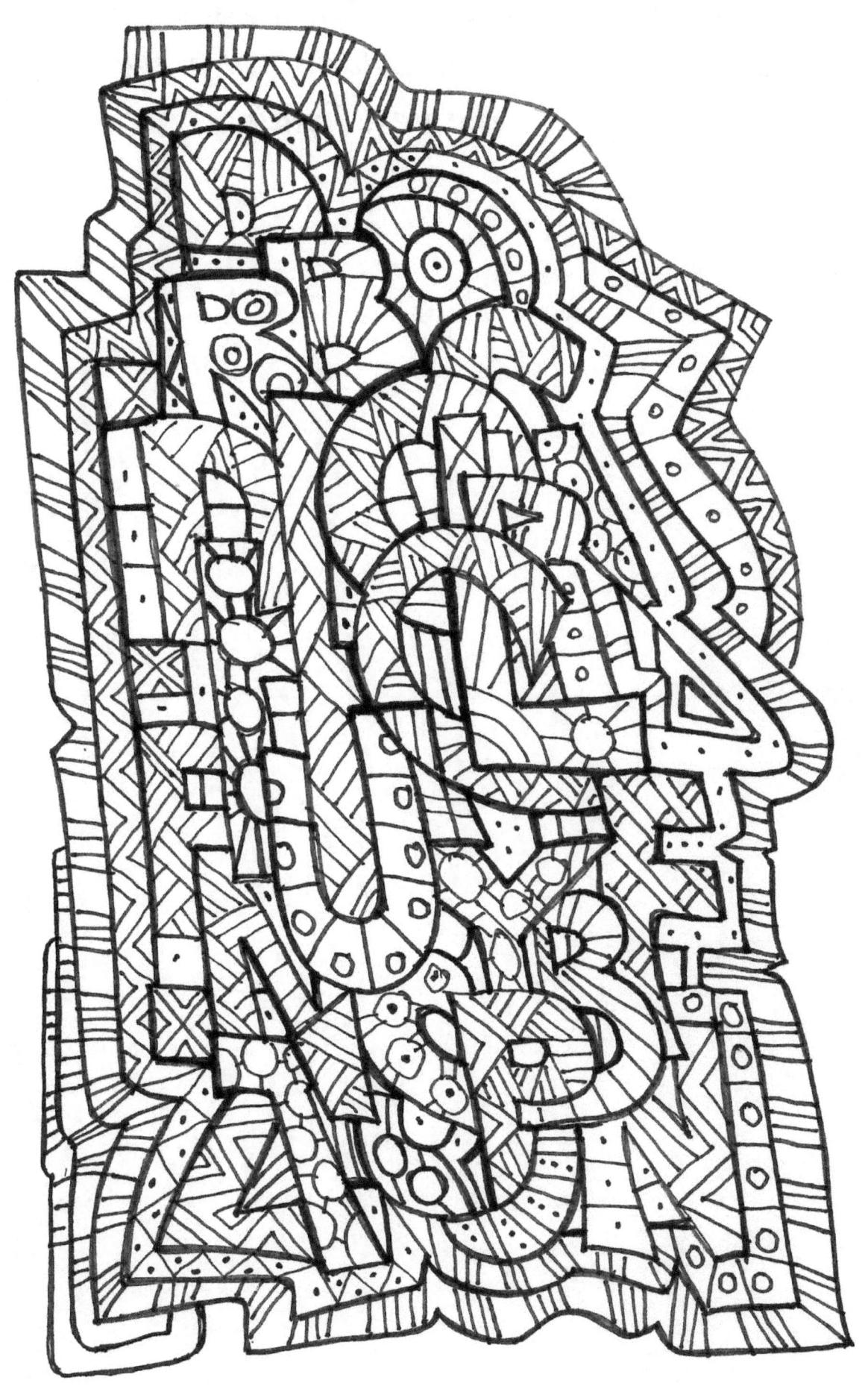

You may wish to place a sheet of paper or poster board under the page you are coloring to prevent damaging the next image.

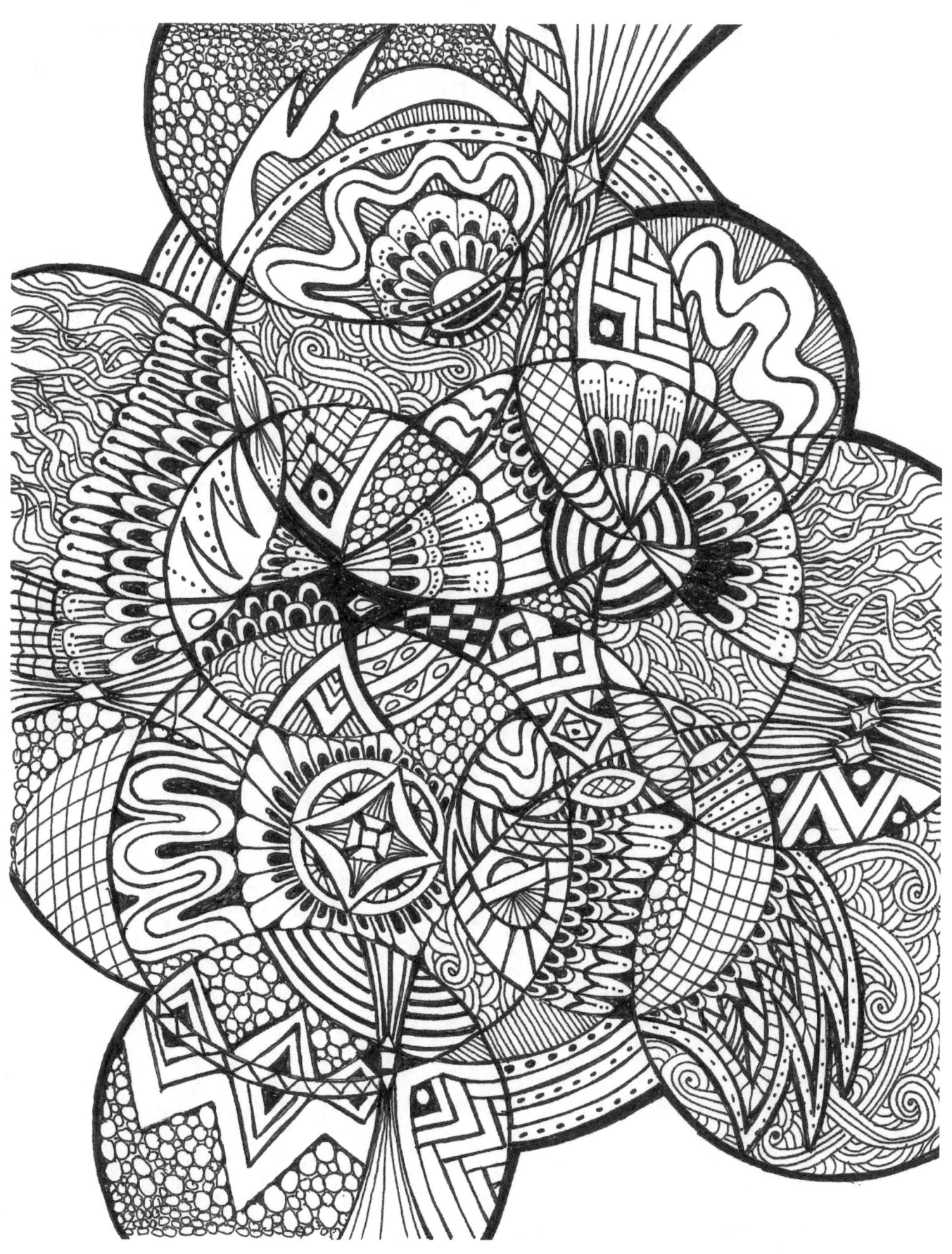

You may wish to place a sheet of paper or poster board under the page you are coloring to prevent damaging the next image.

Thank you for coloring!

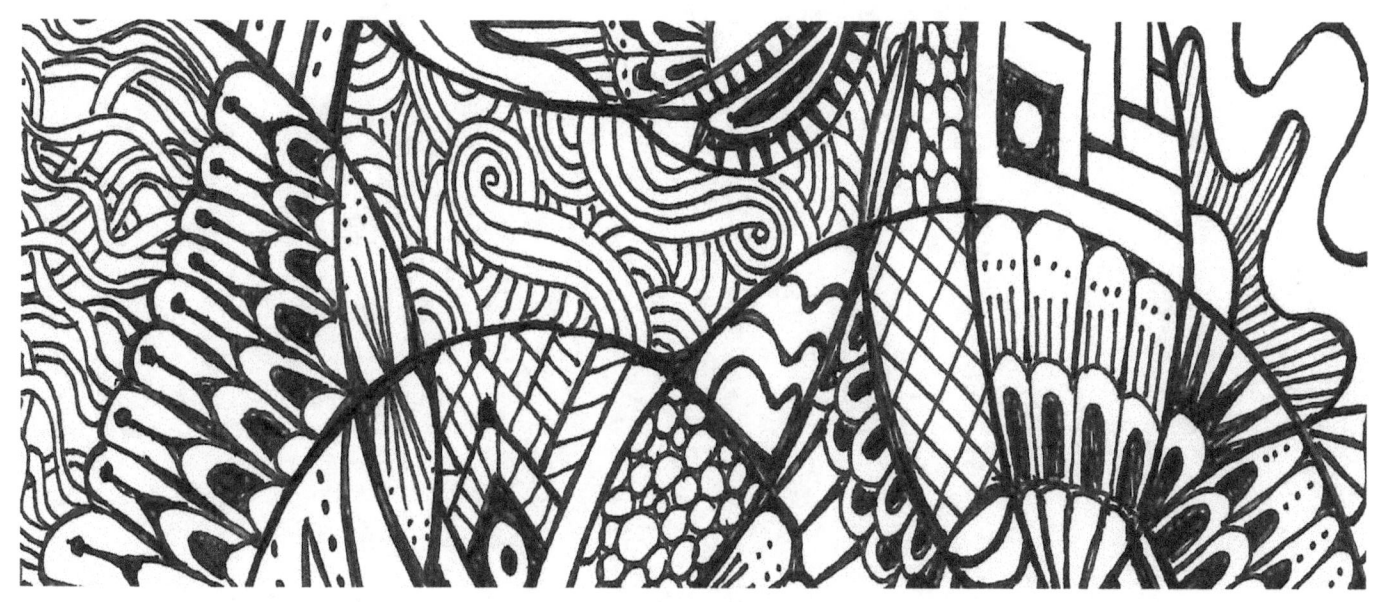

Ten Zone Designs

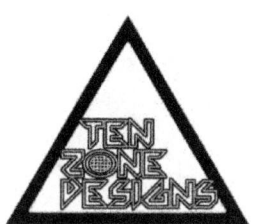

www.ingramcontent.com/pod-product-compliance
Lightning Source LLC
Chambersburg PA
CBHW080709190526

45169CB00006B/2311